Praise for *The Mind of a Conservative Woman*

"In *The Mind of a Conservative Woman*, Senator Blackburn uses important lessons from her own life to inspire future conservative leaders. She knows firsthand one size does not fit all for women when it comes to politics and policy. It's why she encourages young women to do their homework, to ask for advice when they need it, and to choose their battles wisely. This book reminds us why Marsha Blackburn is a role model for so many conservative women."

—Ambassador Nikki Haley, *New York Times* bestselling author of
With All Due Respect: Defending America with Grit and Grace

"Several years ago, I had the privilege of standing alongside Marsha Blackburn in Tennessee's battle against a state income tax. Since then, I've watched with pride as State Senator Blackburn has become U.S. Senator Blackburn. Yet while her platform has expanded, her commitment to conservative values remains as strong as ever. That's the story of her life—and the story of this book."

—Dave Ramsey, bestselling author
and nationally syndicated radio show host

"Has America's Margaret Thatcher emerged from small-town Laurel, Mississippi? That may be what you conclude after reading Tennessee Senator Marsha Blackburn's compelling and entertaining *The Mind of a Conservative Woman*. Part autobiography, part political theory, part self-help for beleaguered conservative women (and men), Blackburn's is the best book by a working politician in years and a must-read for our times."

—Roger L. Simon, prize-winning author,
Academy Award–nominated screenwriter, co-founder of PJ Media,
and Senior Political Columnist of *The Epoch Times*

"Senator Marsha Blackburn is no shrinking violet whose role is to stand beside men, remain silent, and look adoringly and passively while the "boys" do the talking. She's smart, articulate, feisty, and ready to march into hell with a water pistol to fight for what's right. She is not the 'little lady' who makes coffee and cleans up spills—she sits at the head of the table and makes tough decisions. I admire her so much because on issues I care deeply about, she fights harder than anyone I know, and gender has nothing to do with it. Her new book *The Mind of a Conservative Woman* is not meant to soothe, but to rattle. And it does. And it's exactly the kind of leadership that we MUST have in these times when being sweet is for good for tea, but being tough gets the job done in Washington."

—Mike Huckabee, former governor of Arkansas and host of *Huckabee*

"Marsha Blackburn is the real McCoy in every way. Fearless, driven, empathetic, and a true patriot. Through my experiences with her, I've learned she means what she says, and will follow through no matter what it takes. Marsha is an inspiration to me, and is an example not only to American women, but Americans in general as to what it means to 'serve something bigger than yourself' and succeed against all odds. Marsha is the champ!"

—John Rich, award-winning country music artist, songwriter, and entrepreneur

"Marsha's new book is as bold, bright, and fearless as she, and her story as a trailblazer for conservative women in politics is a must-read!"

—Pam Bondi, former Florida attorney general

"*The Mind of a Conservative Woman* sounds a trumpet call to conservative women. With her own amazing rise to the US Senate as a backdrop, Marsha Blackburn encourages and inspires right-thinking women to stop apologizing for who they are, to have confidence in their ideas, and to change the world for the better with their values. It is bold, unapologetic, smart, and feisty. What a book!"

—Andy Puzder, author, Senior Fellow at the Pepperdine University School of Public Policy, and former CEO of CKE Restaurants, Inc.

"People ask me why I'm a big fan of Marsha Blackburn. The reason is that Marsha is a conservative with the same values that I have. In my sport, you look for people that will make a difference—leaders, people who have a winning attitude. These are the qualities Marsha has. I've always said you don't know where you stand until you stand up. Marsha stands up for what she believes, but more importantly she stands up for the people of Tennessee. I campaigned with her when she was running for the Senate. No woman had been a senator from Tennessee before, but she loved the challenge, she worked hard, and she won. Marsha loves the Lord and she's a great mom and devoted wife. She's been successful at everything she's ever done. I'm proud of who she is and proud to call her my friend!"

—Darrell Waltrip, three-time NASCAR Cup Series champion and sports analyst

"Marsha Blackburn has succeeded in everything she has set her mind to—business, politics, marriage, children. Because she makes it look easy, you almost forget that she has had to battle prejudices her entire life, from both the left and the right. Yet Marsha Blackburn never complains; she just smiles and puts one foot in front of the other, which has led her all the way to the United States Senate. This book is a joy to read, the story of a happy warrior driven by a code of integrity, decency, and common sense. It's also a testament to an extraordinary woman. I defy anyone—man or woman—to read this book and NOT come away a committed conservative!"

—K. T. McFarland, former deputy National Security Advisor and author of
#1 bestseller *Revolution: Trump, Washington and "We the People"*

"BPFF—Blond, Petite, Female, Firebrand—only touches the 'seen' of Senator Marsha Blackburn. The unseen embedded deep within her heart is an unwavering commitment to life, liberty, and justice that opens wide the doors of freedom for all. Marsha captures more than just her zeal for truth in *The Mind of a Conservative Woman*. On page after page she empowers women of all backgrounds and ethnicities in seeking and discovering their individual destinies. Her life story epitomizes what she calls conservative faith. *The Mind of a Conservative Woman* is BPFF—Bold, Positive, Frank, Freeing—and I'm happy to call Marsha my friend."

—Star Parker, bestselling author, "Creators" syndicated columnist,
and founder of UrbanCure

"The time for the conservative woman has come, and Senator Marsha Blackburn is at the helm! Marsha is the hallmark of the conservative woman. She has walked the walk and blazed the trail where few women have dared to tread. Having experienced chauvinism and sister cynicism, she has keen insights into overcoming the roadblocks facing the American woman. Marsha is a warrior for women's liberties, but she achieves it in a more challenging, nuanced way—with limited government! In her book, *The Mind of a Conservative Woman*, Marsha underscores the underbelly of feminine liberalism, the irony of big government's mission, and how the mind of the conservative woman is mistaken for genteel, backward weakness. No more! Hear the roar! The conservative woman is rising with reason and victory, and Senator Blackburn's *The Mind of a Conservative Woman* is the handbook for the movement—entertaining, refreshing, encouraging, and rational. Thank you, Marsha!"

—Janine Turner, actress, founder and co-president
of Constituting America

"*The Mind of a Conservative Woman* puts America on notice that the fight for freedom and limited government has a powerful champion in Marsha Blackburn. It lays out a roadmap for others who want to be part of this battle for their country's future. Marsha's book is a must-read for anyone who wants to know how a bold and courageous conservative woman broke through glass ceilings and advanced her principles, all while maintaining the southern charm that makes her one of the Republican party's most effective communicators. Marsha Blackburn helped rewrite the definition of "central casting" when people think about the ideal candidate for Congress. America needs more strong women like Marsha Blackburn. Her book will serve as an inspiration to countless young women who dare to follow in the footsteps of this great conservative trailblazer."

—Congressman Steve Scalise, representative for Louisiana,
Republican Whip, US House of Representatives

"*The Mind of a Conservative Woman* is a must-read for any woman who has been told she can't stand in the public policy arena. Women's achievements deserve to be celebrated and their innovation encouraged. Conservative principles do just that; a new era is upon us. The era of conservative women everywhere."

—Kay C. James, president, The Heritage Foundation, and former director of the Office of Personnel Management

The Mind of a
CONSERVATIVE
WOMAN

The Mind of a
CONSERVATIVE
WOMAN

Seeking the Best for Family and Country

Senator
Marsha Blackburn

WORTHY®

New York • Nashville

Worthy
Hachette Book Group
1290 Avenue of the Americas, New York, NY 10104
worthypublishing.com
twitter.com/worthypub

First Edition: September 2020

Worthy is a division of Hachette Book Group, Inc. The Worthy name and logo are trademarks of Hachette Book Group, Inc.

The publisher is not responsible for websites (or their content) that are not owned by the publisher.

The Hachette Speakers Bureau provides a wide range of authors for speaking events. To find out more, go to www.hachettespeakersbureau.com or call (866) 376-6591.

Print book interior design by Bart Dawson.

Library of Congress Control Number: 2020938829

ISBNs: 978-1-5460-5921-9 (hardcover), 978-1-5460-5920-2 (ebook)

Printed in the United States of America

LSC-C

10 9 8 7 6 5 4 3 2 1

To the conservative women with whom
I've had the honor and pleasure of sharing
public service at the local, state, and federal level.

Contents

Foreword by Newt Gingrich   xv

Introduction: Stop the Madness!   xix

Chapter One: The Stepford Wives of Liberalism   1

Chapter Two: The World That Made Me   16

Chapter Three: How Destinies Turn   30

Chapter Four: A Five-Word Mission   53

Chapter Five: A Noble Heritage   74

Chapter Six: A Noble Heritage—For Women, Too!   101

Chapter Seven: A Caucus of One   123

Chapter Eight: Laws and Sausages   153

Chapter Nine: Public Tactics for the
    Conservative Woman   171

Chapter Ten: Habits of a Lifetime   202

Chapter Eleven: A Hero for Us All   226

Chapter Twelve: A Vision   243

Marsha Blackburn Reading List   245

Acknowledgments   247

Notes   249

Meet a Woman Who Is Changing History

When I first met Marsha Blackburn, I was impressed by her drive, her determination, her intelligence, and her experience. She was clearly someone who was going to make a difference. She had courage and conviction. She also had charm and a great smile. Her entire life had prepared her to lead in Washington.

Marsha came to Washington from a remarkable lifetime of hard work and constant civic involvement. Her enthusiastic energy marked her as a person who enjoyed life and was determined to accomplish something. I did not realize at the time that Marsha had her own company, two children, a great marriage with a supportive husband, and had been both a Republican Party leader and a state senator.

Marsha walked with the determined step of someone who intended to get things done. She was a solid conservative with small-town values and a deep faith commitment (something she maintained in Washington through a Bible study). She was not shaken when others attacked her views. Of course, in Washington a conservative Republican woman in office was not as common as it should have been. The news media wanted to cover liberal women but not conservative women. Marsha understood that and she also understood the power of cheerful persistence. She fought for her beliefs, went to conservative gatherings like CPAC, and became a standout participant in public debates.

Marsha spent eight solidly conservative terms in the United States House of Representatives (2002–2016). She was a valuable member of the House Republican team and built a network of strong friends and supporters among her Republican colleagues.

Then in 2018 Marsha took a big gamble. When Senator Bob Corker, the chair of the Senate Foreign Relations Committee, decided to retire, Marsha determined that she would run for the Senate. At first the Senate race appeared to be an uphill challenge. Former governor Phil Bredesen, widely respected and with a great reputation as a pro-business moderate Democrat, was as formidable as any Democratic Senate candidate in the country.

Clearly, Bredesen's statewide name recognition as a former governor gave him an advantage. Marsha's initial base was limited to only one congressional district. And the stakes were high. Senator Mitch McConnell became deeply involved in the race because he knew the Senate Republican majority was narrow and that Bredesen was exactly the kind of Democrat who could help his party take back the Senate. Still, Marsha was unswerving, having been a Tea Party Republican, a solid conservative, and a strong supporter of President Donald Trump.

The big turning point may have come when Democrats decided to smear Judge Brett Kavanaugh and attempt to destroy his reputation. Marsha, like most Republicans and many independents, was appalled at the viciousness and the dishonesty that the liberal media and the Democrats used to try to destroy someone just for being conservative. The Kavanaugh fight was decisive in Marsha's Senate race. It galvanized Republican voters and made them so angry that they flooded to the polls. In a Trump state (he had carried Tennessee by a

650,000 vote margin—with 60.7% of the vote, the largest margin since 1972) there were a lot of Republicans to be roused into taking a stand.

Marsha captured the essence of the campaign when she asked, "Do you think Phil Bredesen would vote with crying Chuck Schumer or would he vote with our president when it comes to supporting our troops and supporting our veterans?" This clear contrasting of liberal versus conservative elected Marsha handily with 54.7% of the vote. She carried all but three counties in Tennessee.

Marsha is a major force in the Senate and in America. She is also an inspiration to young women who would like to go into public service. *The Mind of a Conservative Woman* is a good place for them to start. It gives them a chance to get to know someone who is going to be playing an ever-bigger role in America's future.

—Newt Gingrich, former Speaker of the House
and architect of the Contract with America

Stop the Madness!

The year was 2002 and I was preparing to run for the U.S. Congress. To be as informed as I could be before I declared my candidacy, I spoke to as many people as possible about the challenges I would face and the skills it would take to win. I have remembered one particular conversation from that time ever since.

I was talking to a gentleman who was well connected politically, a man known for being a savvy insider. We were discussing the slate of candidates I would face in my run for office when he said that one of these candidates was direct from central casting, that he looked and behaved in exactly the way that you would expect of a congressman.

What he meant was that the man was tall and good-looking and had that 1950s movie "distinguished gentleman" hair. I had to admit that the man did look the part—if the world were populated only by males and political decisions were made based on looks alone.

I looked this savvy politico dead in the eye and asked him exactly what he meant by his comment. He was stunned by my question. Then he caught himself. He sat silently and said nothing more.

I was dismayed but not surprised. You see, I am blond and petite. I grew up in Mississippi and my accent still surfaces from time and time. I make no apologies for that. And did I mention that I am a woman? Of course, it never crossed this gentleman's mind that I might be the one from central casting. It never occurred to him that members of the U.S. Congress might come in blond, southern, petite, female packages.

It also never occurred to him that as I stood before him I represented a wealth of experience most men don't have. I had started and run my own business, led at least a dozen non-profit organizations, served in the Tennessee legislature, and led some of the fiercest political battles in my state's history.

All these years later, I've grown accustomed to such biases. I wish I could tell you, now that I have been elected to the U.S. Senate, that the situation has changed. It hasn't. I'm still told that I can't win, can't lead, and can't succeed because I'm too much of one thing or another—or not enough of one thing or another.

It doesn't seem to matter that I've taken on some of the most controversial causes in American public life and have often won—causes like the battles for women, for life, for the men and women in our armed forces, and for privacy rights, to name but a few. It also doesn't matter that I am an outspoken American statesman in a dangerous world and a strife-ridden Washington, DC, and I am still standing. Beyond all this, I've been threatened with rape for what I believe. I've been threatened with murder. I've been told that members of my family would be harmed.

Yet because I look as I do and have the background that I do—and because I am a woman—I just don't fit the central casting image required to make a difference in our age. At least, that's what they say.

Now, let me tell you even worse news. I am a conservative woman. It is a shocking confession, I know, but it is true! I realize this sets me apart from much of the thinking that prevails in American politics. I don't care. My conscience and my convictions rule. My vision for my nation and my life is not mired in statism and government control. I am not in lockstep with the socialist political left in America. I am not among the

Stepford Wives of liberalism. I'll dare to say it again: I am a conservative woman.

I realize what this means to the ill informed. To this crowd, the phrase "conservative woman" is nearly the same as "rich bitch," "country club Barbie," and "leggy lobotomized lemming." None of it is true, of course, but these are just some of the insults I expect to be thrown at any woman who has broken from the politically correct pack—because they have been said of me.

Part of the reason that I am so familiar with the taunts and the jibes is that I live in Tennessee but work in Washington, DC. In Washington, DC, conservative women are fourth-class citizens at best. If the media wants an interview, for example, they go first to men or women who are members of the Democratic Party. Then they go to Republican men. A conservative woman is the last on their list—unless, of course, their point is to show that she is out of touch or a holdover from a bygone era.

The left can't believe that a female could actually choose *not* to be a member of the National Organization for Women, that they might be pro-life, or that they might stand for conservative and constitutional values. They can't believe that you don't need the federal government to lead you through life, holding your hand and providing for you—cradle to grave.

The media and the DC establishment are stunned that conservative women even exist, much less that they dare to speak their minds.

We do exist, though, and I'll tell you why. It is because most American women want freedom. They are as independent in their political thinking as they are unique in their lifestyles, and they ought to be. They aren't primarily loyal to either major political party in this country. They are loyal to ideas and to values, to traditions and the things they love. They want the freedom to live out all of this to the full.

They want to rise as high as their gifts will carry them. They want government to be limited, accountable, and only as large as it needs to be. They also want government to fulfill its promises, to be led by responsible and respectful politicians, and to be out of the way so that American women don't have to think about public policy issues every minute of the day.

Women want safe communities, control of their own health care, fairness in American public life, and to keep more of their money in their own pockets. The majority of American women want economic security, national security, an end to abortion and to war, more say in their children's education, and freedom for whatever religion they practice.

Put another way, the average woman simply wants more control over her own life. And she deserves it. She doesn't need

Washington, DC, to decide what her child learns in the classroom, how many hours she can work every week, or how she negotiates her schedule with her employer. She is busy with work, family, friends, and care for herself, and she would like for government to get the heck out of the way.

This isn't radical feminism. This isn't a bra-burning, man-hating, children-resenting, bitter-edged approach to life and politics. No. Good women love life, love their men, and are lovingly devoted to their children. They also love their bras! What they want is the freedom to be the magnificent creatures they are made to be.

Liberalism, with its statist solutions and bloated government programs, is the opposite of the freedom women seek. Liberalism sets women in opposition to every other identity group in American society. It pits the needs of women against the needs of, say, Hispanics, and the needs of working mothers against the needs of immigrants, for example. Rather than grow the grand American experience of prosperity for all, liberalism creates a bitter, snarling, grasping war of interest groups that serves no one well and that makes us all morally smaller, less visionary human beings.

Conservatism stands against all of this. As conservative founding father William Buckley once said, conservatism "stands athwart history, yelling 'Stop!'" Stop the crushing growth of government, stop the destructive intrusions of the swollen state, stop the stifling of the individual, stop the madness of identity politics and the never-ending rush to feed at the pork barrel buffet that is the manipulating tool of liberalism.

Instead, here is what conservativism says to women: You are amazing beings. You have been made in the image of an awesome God who has fashioned you to achieve gloriously in this life. You are smart, you are capable, you are talented, you are wise, and you are able to do magnificent things. What you want, and what conservatism promises, is a welcoming arena for your gifts, is the fairness and protection you need to rise brilliantly. Government has its role in your life, but that role should be kept minimal by the smart constitutional checks and balances crafted by our founding fathers. Armed with this knowledge, go be the inspiring beings you are made to be.

This is the promise of conservativism. This is why I am a conservative woman. This is also what the following pages are all about. It is time for the mind of the conservative woman to be understood, to be celebrated, and to be passed on as a legacy for generations of women yet to come. It is time for the emptiness of liberalism to be exposed and for the conditions that make for female achievement to be proclaimed wherever women toil and dream. It is time for conservative women to no longer be regarded as the fourth-class people they have been seen to be, but for these bravehearts to step out boldly on behalf of women everywhere, on behalf of all that God has intended the women of the world to become.

The moment of the conservative woman has arrived. Come with me as we make history together.

Chapter One

The Stepford Wives of Liberalism

The year was 2012. Barack Obama was running for a second presidential term against Mitt Romney and by May of that year the battle had become fierce. A contentious theme was the "war on women," the claim that Republican opposition to abortion, to government overreach, and to creeping socialism was a not-so-veiled war against the women of America. To raise the stakes in this political fight, the Obama campaign issued an internet slideshow entitled "The Life of Julia." It was, let me tell you, everything that is wrong with liberalism's vision for women.

You can find this slide show on YouTube today. Handle with care! So misguided was this bit of media and the perspective on women it extolled that even *The Atlantic* magazine proclaimed in a headline that "Obama's 'Life of Julia' Was Made to Be Mocked."[1] I couldn't agree more. So let's get to it!

Julia, a cartoon character, is apparently meant to be an American everywoman, at least as Obama's extremist vision perceives her. We follow her from the age of three to the age of sixty-seven. There are no parents, no friends, no husband, no church, and no community that play a significant role in Julia's story. No, her only meaningful relationship is the state. It is government that grants what she needs, government that makes her life possible.[2]

At the age of three, Julia is enrolled in the Head Start program. We are told this is thanks to "steps President Obama has taken." It doesn't seem to matter that Head Start was founded in 1965 when Obama was four years old. When Julia is seventeen, her high school becomes part of the Race to the Top program, a federal fund for spurring innovation in public schools. The next year, when Julia is eighteen, her family qualifies for an Opportunity Tax Credit. The insinuation all through this story is that government is making Julia who she is.

She goes to college and later pays her loans off only through the largesse, once again, of Barack Obama, who graciously chose to cap income-based federal student-loan payments. At the age of twenty-two, Julia needs surgery, which is paid for by Barack Obama's health care law. Of course, mean old Mitt Romney would have struck down that law and abandoned Julia. Thank God for the government and Barack Obama.

When Julia graduates from college, she decides to pursue her career as a web designer—but only because "her health insurance is required to cover birth control and preventive care, letting Julia focus on her work rather than worry about her health." Blessed be the State that frees us from worry! Blessed be our father in Washington!

Julia then turns thirty-one and "decides to have a child." There is no mention of a father or even a sperm donor. Julia just decides. Where does she get this child? Whole Foods? Thankfully, Julia's son, Zachary, is off to a great start in life because he attends a Race to the Top–funded public school. Praise be yet again to Barack Obama.

When Julia is forty-two, she gets a small business loan, and we are told this is due to "President Obama's tax cuts for small businesses." I should point out that according to the slide-show's chronology, Julia is forty-two in the year 2044. Barack Obama is now eighty-three years old and is in his ninth term as president. Clearly, the slideshow hoped that King Obama would reign for generations to come, "standing up for women throughout their lives."

Yet the federally fashioned life of Julia is not yet over. At sixty-seven, she is able to retire and all due to Social Security and Medicare which grant her peace and allow her to volunteer in a "community garden" for the rest of her life.

It is all a federal fantasy, a happily-ever-after tale designed to delight the socialist heart. Yet there is little of reality in it.

Nowhere are we told that Head Start has failed to significantly improve elementary education. We are not told that Medicare and Social Security are careening toward insolvency. We are also not told that Julia's share of the national debt is rocketing upward and will continue to rise throughout her life. The fictions in this tale are numerous, and I could devote the rest of this book to the false vision, false promises, and false facts coded in the Julia story.

Yet here is what angers me about Obama's tale of Julia and most all of liberalism's vision: What does it say about women? What does it say about the skill, the ingenuity, the genius, and the sheer power of women? The answer is "Absolutely nothing!"

You see, if Julia is any indication, the pitiful American woman is too weak and stupid to handle life on her own. Her parents can't save and manage insurance well enough to take care of their children. Our average woman inherits this incompetence. She can't go to college, can't start a business, and can't handle a simple surgery without Washington, DC, taking her by the hand. Clearly, she also can't save, can't prosper, and can't invest so as to care for herself. She can't even manage her own birth control. She then works her whole life but still has to rely entirely on government programs in order to retire. It is a dim vision straight out of the Marxist canon, but it is the assumption that women must eternally be bumbling wards of the state that incenses me.

We are better than this. As a nation. As women. As the human race. We are better than what liberalism portrays.

Nowhere in this liberal bedtime story is the private sector to be found. Nowhere is anyone creating, investing, and prospering. Nowhere does community play a role. Nowhere is there even a husband or a friend to make a difference. Nowhere is there faith in God and in the American mechanisms that have produced such wealth and freedom in the world. No, apparently the primary relationship of the American woman is government. She is the government's to have and to hold. She belongs to government until death does them part.

It is no wonder that "The Life of Julia" was so roundly mocked when it first appeared. Using the hashtag #Julia, Twitter exploded in condescension. More than a few mothers wrote that they would use "The Life of Julia" to teach their daughters how *not* to live their lives. One popular tweet noted how Julia's whole life seemed to be about waiting at her mailbox for "Obama cash."[3]

I despise this stifling vision of womanhood. I despise also the insistence of liberalism that all women must align with this definition of who women are. I resist it. I stand against it. I refuse to be one of the Stepford Wives of liberalism.

You know the movie I'm talking about, don't you? It first appeared in 1972. It was based on the thriller of the same name by Ira Levin, the famous novelist and playwright who also gave us *A Kiss Before Dying*, *The Boys from Brazil*, *Rosemary's Baby*, and the popular play *Deathtrap*.

In *The Stepford Wives*, Levin gives us a fictional community in Connecticut in which the men have conspired together to replace their human wives with compliant, docile, ever-willing robots. Clearly, the men in the town of Stepford prefer obedient machines to living, breathing human beings with minds and hearts of their own. When the movie first appeared in 1972, it was a big hit that led to widespread discussion about the role of women in the world, and this first film gave birth to a remake in 2004 starring Nicole Kidman, Bette Midler, and Glenn Close.

The heart of the movie's message was that some people,

some cultures, would rather have rigid, goose-stepping confor-mity than the challenges and blessings that come from allowing people to think for themselves and express themselves freely. I'm sorry to tell you that American liberalism today is one of those cultures in which conformity is prized and individual-ity is punished. That is why I say that I refuse to be among the Stepford Wives of liberalism.

Nowhere is the straitjacket of liberal conformity more evi-dent than in the leftist talking points heard on nearly every news talk show today. I'm always amused when a cable news outlet runs a slate of twelve liberal talking heads saying the same things in the same phrases and all using the same inflec-tions. It often seems that Democrats, who are institutionalists, insist upon using the same old lineup of talkers, all of whom have been given the same talking points. Most of the conser-vatives I know are individualists who make their points using different words and different analogies, all through different personalities who are not from the town of Stepford.

Now, there are indeed times I wish that we could get all Republicans saying the same words in the same way. That's just not how conservatives work, though. It's also not how freedom works. Our team simply wants to say and do things in their own unique way. That's what makes them conservatives.

Liberalism's prison-like conformity does not just manifest

itself in the media; it also rears its ugly head on the floor of Congress. I cannot tell you how many times, while serving in the House, I watched my friends across the aisle and wondered how long it took them to journey from their hometown of Stepford. When they form a dance line down the aisle of the House, stepping to the microphone and repeating the same tired sentences, one right after the other, you can't help but wonder where it is exactly that the Democrats replace human beings with robots. Is there a hidden facility underground somewhere? Are federal funds used for this procedure? You can't help but think these thoughts when all the Democratic women dress in the same color in protest of a policy. There seems to be conformity without consciousness, performance without a pulse. Style over substance. It is the same when women of the left all decide to wear that symbolic pink cap. They aren't helping themselves. They aren't gaining strength in numbers. They merely reveal that they have all undergone the same Stepford transformation.

It is pretty much the same with the National Organization for Women. This bunch has spent decades trying to convince women that they can't achieve anything on their own and that they need laws on the books that provide carveouts and safe harbors. They shout loudly that it is the government's role to be their protector and give them a step up on the ladder of success. Yet most women I know want to get government out of the way. What they ask for is a level playing field and a chance to get in the game. They will achieve on their own. They are confident they can rise to the top. They aren't pitiful little women who need government to artificially give them a place in the world. They'll make their own place, thank you. Just give them the chance.

Honestly, I don't think most women on the political left stop to think long enough or deep enough about how shallow they appear by parroting the talking points of some left-wing advocacy group. It is even more curious to me when they get on the bandwagon to advocate for taking away some of their own rights and then argue that these rights should be given to government. We all know that anytime government steps in to fill a void or provide a service, not only is there a dollar cost, there is also the opportunity cost of having responsibility taken away and thus having freedoms taken away as well.

The cradle-to-grave, government-controlled lifestyle of "Julia" from the Obama years was a bit of a head-scratcher. Do you really want to rely on the feds for your education, career, health care, retirement? Do you not want to make those decisions for yourself? The answer from most women is "Of course I want to make those decisions. I'm smart, informed, independent, and motivated. I want people to have opportunity and be fulfilled in their lives, but I don't need the federal government in charge of my choices." This is how most women think and feel: "Just leave me be," as we say in the South.

Yet this is not what the political left in America has in mind for you. For as much talk about women's empowerment as comes from them, what they deliver are merely talking points and dictates. The implication is "Do as we say, and if we feel that you ever disagree with us we will publicly call you out and shame you." When they finish, you will not recognize yourself. It is their way of getting back at women who do not subscribe to their liberal doctrine.

Think about outstanding conservative women who have crossed your path. I would imagine you have watched the left-leaning media rip them to shreds. I know I have been the target of this kind of treatment time and again. Still, conservative women refuse to conform, refuse to become the Stepford Wives of liberalism, so the left has no use for them. It is almost as though they are saying, "No woman can be a real woman if she disagrees with the talking points of the left!"

———————————

Now, the approach of conservative women is entirely different. I know because I am one of them. Conservative women do not need a set of talking points to frame what they believe.

What they believe is a part of their being, and they are good at evaluating the issues of the day against their principles. There is no daily women's television show or women's march that is going to abruptly change their bedrock values. They observe. They take in the facts. They talk the issues over with a few friends. They then apply what they have learned from experience, family, and faith. They draw conclusions.

Afterward, well, most of them keep their thoughts to themselves. They aren't contentious. They don't feel the need to press a case or become the one everyone avoids at the company cafeteria or the community charity event. They leave the love of blowups to left-leaning women. The conservative women I know are confident, productive, centered, and quiet. I admit that sometimes I wish conservative women made a bit more noise in the public square, especially when I'm out there taking hits for conservative values in Washington, but it just isn't the way women of the right are. They aren't angry. They don't feel the need to be loud. Their confidence about their values gives them inner strength, not a need for outer drama. Putting "pussy hats" on their heads would only diminish them, as it does the women of the left—whether they know it or not.

This more elegant, reserved approach of conservative women came naturally to me through my family upbringing and culture, Christian values, and the example of women I admire. One moment from my college career has always symbolized this for me. When I was a student at Mississippi State University, I was the president of the Associated Women Students. I remember that in this role I had the opportunity to attend a women's student government convention in Chicago. I sat near the stage and attended every session so I could learn and absorb as much as possible. I wanted to take back every good idea, every helpful morsel of knowledge, to help the female students on my campus.

It so happened that Gloria Steinem was a featured speaker. When she was introduced, that room full of young women leapt to their feet with excitement. I sat in my chair. I did not agree with her position on issues. I did not agree with her that women would be better off with government having more control of our lives. I admit that she was a compelling speaker. I could understand her appeal and how she and her crew have built such a strong movement through the years.

Yet I simply disagreed with her. Notice, though, that my big act of dissent was simply to stay in my seat when she was introduced. I did not yell out in opposition to her expounding ideas I deeply disagreed with. I did not charge the stage. I did not throw a pie. I did not maneuver to get myself arrested. Instead, I listened. I sharpened my arguments in opposition. I made my case as widely as I could when I returned to school. I am still making my case today. No antics. No dishonor. No absurd wardrobe required.

Now, contrast this with the first time I ever experienced someone raising their voice at me in a public setting because they disagreed with me. I'll never forget it. It was 1992 and I had just won a Republican primary race for a congressional seat. I was attending a charity function in Tennessee. A woman walked right up to me, wineglass in hand, and proceeded to berate me for choosing to run for a "man's job." She was sure, she said, that my children and husband needed me to be home. She told me, as if I didn't already know, that I had young children at home and that I should be more responsible. She said all this at full volume, obviously hoping that everyone in attendance would hear.

I calmly made the point that I chose to run because I wanted my children to live in a world that cherishes freedom, that lets them grow up to dream big dreams and make those dreams come true. She was not endeared by this. She proceeded to raise her voice again, making it known that she was a Democrat, that she did not agree with me on the issues, and that I did not have her support. People who were standing near were stunned that she would act in such a way in a public setting.

In my fantasy life, I punched her right in her overpowdered

nose. That's not how it went in reality, though. Instead, I thanked her for the "conversation" and moved on to enjoy my evening. There was no sense trying to reason with the unreasonable— or the rude.

The only hope I had of changing that woman's mind was to be what she was not. I showed restraint. I listened. I was kind. Clearly she just did not like the idea of a conservative woman breaking a barrier, accomplishing something she could not or would not. In her frustration and resentment, she chose to strike out at what she sensed would be a core value for me: care for my family and home.

Notice her motivation. Frustration and resentment.

Notice her method. Shame.

Notice her tactics. Rudeness and public posturing.

This was not just this woman's manner. This is too often the manner of the women of the political left.

I am not perfect in such situations, but in that particular moment I was guided by the character and control born of my values. I was also probably guided by generations of well-mannered southern ancestors who were peering over my shoulder just then. I take no credit. This is simply the grace that comes to us from our conservative values. It is grace that makes us individuals. It is grace that elevates us, I believe. It is grace that frees us from the need for adolescent demonstrations and allows us to be the noble women of dignity we are meant to be.

Now I say all this to contrast the average conservative woman with the Stepford minions of the left. I do not want to live "the Life of Julia." Nor do you. I do not want to be a Stepford Wife of liberalism. Nor do you. I also do not want to be married to the state or believe of myself that I can achieve nothing unless Washington steps in. I will not be reduced by liberal talking points, by liberal shaming, by liberal definitions of who I am, and by liberal disregard of what God has made me to be.

It is time for a gentle but transforming revolution in this country. It is time for American women to cast off the shackles of liberal dogma and adopt a philosophy of freedom that will change our land and leave our daughters a vision and a nation worthy of them.

Julia was a cartoon, a figment of the Obama campaign's imagination and liberalism's constraints. Let's leave her to her Stepford, statist, cartoon world. Out here in reality, millions of capable, skilled, fierce women are making the conservative philosophy of freedom their own—and are ready to take the lead. I want to help them. I want to teach them what I know. I want to see the day of promise for American women fulfilled.

Chapter Two

The World That Made Me

There are many ways that people arrive at conservatism. Sometimes just reading a thoughtful book or hearing a single insightful speech by a Ronald Reagan or a Margaret Thatcher or a great thinker like Russell Kirk or Milton Friedman will start the process. Others first confront conservative thought in their high school or college years when they read the works of Edmund Burke or Nathaniel Hawthorne or Alexis de Tocqueville. A few even come to it on their own, after seeing the devastations of socialism and envisioning a world of liberty, of limited government, of free markets, and of individual character and responsibility.

All these paths are valid. All have produced great minds and leaders. Yet my path was different. Conservatism was woven into the everyday world that made me. From the soil of my youth and the dinner table conversations I knew as a child, from the example of parents and the warm values of a loving southern community, I came naturally to what I believe today and to what I most hold dear. I cannot tell you how grateful I am.

Wherever I go in life, whatever heights I might achieve, I carry Laurel, Mississippi, with me. This is where I began. You may have become familiar with my town through the hit HGTV show called *Home Town*, which is all about Laurel. As the hosts launch out into ever-new renovation adventures, you get to see the lovely place that was my first home.

Laurel is an unusual town and has an unusual history. It is important to know that it sits in Jones County, which was made famous by a rebellion during the Civil War led by a man named Newton Knight. Along with a band of like-minded white men in southern Mississippi, Knight waged guerrilla warfare against the Confederacy and declared the entire county the Free State of Jones. Some historians contend that the county actually seceded from the Confederacy. Blacks were welcomed and declared free. Called "Knight's Company," a force of 125 fought Confederate troops and drove Confederate government out of Jones County. You may have seen this fascinating story depicted in the movie *Free State of Jones*, starring Matthew McConaughey.

The Laurel of my youth was, as it is today, a charming place. I have often said that "Laurel likes pretty." Though the whole county barely numbers fifty thousand people, the town of Laurel is a city of the arts. It boasts the Lauren Rogers Museum of Art, and there are regular concert series and Little Theatre art shows. The community is close-knit and takes pride in every flower box and tree, every bit of heritage and sign of progress.

It was said in my childhood home that Dad made the living but Mother made it worthwhile. My father sold oil field production equipment all his life and so was part of Laurel's two main industries: oil and lumber. He had served in World War II and returned home with all the values and habits of that heroic generation. He was passionately patriotic, loved the American flag, saw political involvement as the great duty and privilege of citizens, and spoke of faith and freedom as nearly the meaning of life. He was also intensely frugal, hardworking, and given to quiet, honorable ways. His name was Hilman Wedgeworth, and I adored him then as I do now.

In her later years my feisty mother dared to laughingly proclaim that she had always been the "household executive" in our house. It was true. This amazing lady not only cared for her husband and three children and kept a beautiful, well-ordered home, but she gave herself to every cause that won her heart. I remember that she was always volunteering. It was what a lot of folks did back then, but she took this devotion to new heights. Efforts at church, in civic clubs, in arts organizations, and in strategies to help the hurting always won her. She is a dynamo of generosity, and I'm thankful that her example is forever embedded in my heart.

It is hard for some of my young friends to understand this today, but my childhood universe was filled with maxims that were constantly reinforced by my family and by my wider community. It sounds corny now, I suppose, but there were pithy, powerful statements that I must have heard thousands of times in my life, words that penetrated the soul and shaped character.

Give back more than you take.
Leave things in better shape than you find them.
Clean up behind yourself.
Be resourceful.
Be helpful and kind.

Go to church with open ears and heart and with helping hands.

Don't be idle—an idle mind is the devil's workshop.

I absorbed these and dozens of other principles as I moved
through my childhood, taking them in with the ease of breathing and with trusting acceptance. I heard them first at home.
They were not preached so much as explained by my parents.
It was not uncommon for an entire suppertime conversation
to be gently devoted to exploring a principle of character. My
parents would pick up the theme and explain what God and
faith and principles of character had to do with daily life, how
society works best when its people are moral and devoted
to good.

These truths formed my family culture, but they also
echoed from nearly every experience I had with friends and
neighbors in Laurel. When I went to church, to my 4-H Club
meeting, to school, and to dozens of other activities, I heard
these same lessons, this same vision of society and personal
conduct, restated and reapplied over and over again. It was not
wearisome to me. It seemed that the adult world was preparing
us for life, that a caring community was eager to show us the
wise path.

Yet as much as simple words of commonsense wisdom

filled my days, most of what I acquired during my early years was absorbed almost without thought. When you are busy with living life, you aren't necessarily aware that your worldview, values, and principles of conduct are being molded. You don't feel it. It doesn't come with careful observation. You drink it in. You adopt it effortlessly. This was true of my early life in Laurel. I saw a way of life, attitudes and priorities, lived out. I made them my own. That was the way it happened. You learn what you live. It's the living that is the lesson, that determines who you are. It all seems in retrospect to have been almost automatic. This doesn't mean it didn't come with great effort on the part of my parents and the people in my community. It also doesn't mean that I mastered it all perfectly. It simply means that I was shaped by a culture more than formal lessons, by truths lived out more than by words pressed upon me.

This meant I didn't have to come to an epiphany later in life. I entered later life with solid certainties that I have with me to this day. I walked with a living God. My heart was filled with a faith that defined my days. I loved my country and was grateful for all the devotion and sacrifice that allowed me to be an American. I was eager to help my fellow man. It's what Christians do. It's what good people do. It's what Americans do. By way of serving God, country, and my fellow man, I strove to be a good citizen. Helping to build a good society would achieve much good in the world and drive off much evil. You could draw a line in my family between serving God and voting, between loving people and voicing your opinion. It was all interconnected, all part of the same fabric woven of faith, civic duty, and love.

As I look back upon my early life now, every activity seemed to play a role in maturing my understanding of the world and clarifying my place in it. For example, each week my family would make a trip to the town library. This may sound like a sweet, small-town thing to do, yet it produced a revolution. I couldn't wait for these visits, and the idea that I could take armfuls of books home for free was thrilling to me. I had loved reading from an early age, and what I delighted in most were biographies and autobiographies. I remember very clearly reading about Clara Barton, Benjamin Franklin, Thomas Jefferson, and dozens of others. I pondered the lives of these giants. I wondered about what they were really like, how the fires of greatness were awakened, and how they overcame pain and challenge.

I remember like it was yesterday being ten years old and musing about these titans. I was reading about what my own life was going to be like. *What are my gifts? What do I have to give? Where can I make a difference?* These were often my childhood reflections, and it was because my reading and the lofty virtues of my family and Laurel constantly pressed these thoughts into my mind.

Often my reading and my mother's maxims blended into potent life lessons. My parents frequently said that there are two kinds of people in the world: people of wealth and people of prominence. They said that people of character almost always become prominent because their goal would be to improve the lives of others. Yet people of wealth aren't necessarily people of character. Sometimes wealthy people don't give of their means and are completely self-absorbed. They said that I should strive to be a person of character. It would lead to prominence and then to whatever wealth I was meant to have.

This truth helped to color the lenses through which I viewed the world. There were others. In fact, there were two principles that were nearly our family creed. We recited them often and worked hard to live them out. The first of these was "Give back more than you take." My mother provided the most practical example of this I've ever seen. If she borrowed a pie plate or a dish of some kind, she never returned it empty. A borrowed pie plate would be returned with a pie, a dish adorned by some tasty thank-you gift or a beautiful flower from her garden. She always enhanced, always gave back more, always made sure there was "value added," as we say today. This was a way of life, in every pursuit and on every occasion possible.

The second family principle was "Leave things in better shape than you find them." One of my most unusual childhood memories is of my family going out to clean up roadways. We picked up bottles, filled huge bags of trash, and sometimes would even plant trees and trim grass. I remember my parents saying, "I don't want to drive by here every day and look at trash." This was their way of living the family principle: Leave the world better than you found it. In other words, always make things better. This is a way of life for me now.

It is obvious looking back all these years later that God used my reading, my mother's gentle lessons, and the reinforcement of my community to craft me into the person I would become. I remember that I was in the fifth grade when we had a reading competition. My teacher, Mrs. Loper, announced that there would be prizes for the student who read the most books. Now, I confess that I am a seriously competitive person. I want to be the best, and while I won't harm anyone to get to the top, I will kill myself to achieve. Needless to say, I was determined to win. I decided to try to read every book in our classroom library.

I'm not sure what possessed me other than pure competitive spirit, yet I remember that I filled every minute with turning even a few pages of a book on my list. Thankfully, the top shelf of our library corner was filled with biographies of prominent people who had played significant roles in history. Most were men, but some were female. I read them all. Somewhere along the way, this ceased being just a competition and became an adventure. The exploits of the people I read about became vividly alive in my mind. I cheered when they overcame adversity; I felt their dark nights of the soul and their victories.

I was changed by this. There was an impartation. My reading instilled in me a transforming desire to use my energies to make life better for others. That was what Lincoln had done. That was what Eleanor Roosevelt had done and hundreds of others. I wanted to do this as well. When the competition ended, I finished at the top and won Mrs. Loper's praise. It was gratifying. Yet something more had happened. I had secretly begun nurturing a new understanding of myself. I knew that there was more that I could do in my life than I had ever dreamed. I could choose to make it so. That was what the great men and women had done, and that was what I now understood that I had the power to do also.

My teachers played a huge role in unpacking this new understanding of myself. They opened doors for me and encouraged me to explore beyond the physical boundaries of my little world. Sometimes this was done with the smallest gesture or comment. Once after I had read aloud to my class, Mrs. Loper commented that I read well publicly and that she hoped I'd make books a cherished part of my life. It was just a sentence or two, but often that is all it takes to awaken part of a child's destiny.

A little later, in high school, I took a Latin class taught by Mrs. Kidder. The power of language began to open up to me. I began to understand what language can do in the human soul. I learned the roots of words and how these roots reveal meaning. I fell in love with the English language and came to see how the right word in the right context could be a thing of strength and persuasion and beauty.

As the editor of the high school yearbook during this time, I was constantly writing and creating. I hungered to be a skilled writer, to use a few words to say a great deal and to change minds and hearts by what I put on paper. That Latin class and the demands of writing for the yearbook energized me and prepared me for much that I would do in the future.

Once I had a sense of potential ignited in my soul, every experience seemed to conspire to prepare me for my future. During all my youth, I was deeply involved in 4-H, the program that dates back to the 1920s and that helps young people learn innovative farming through hands-on experience. The 4-H name stands for Head, Heart, Hands, and Health. It was a huge part of my youth and my training for future life. I was a proud 4-H Club scholarship winner, and so I was invested in myriad projects kids today might find humorous. I judged horticulture competitions. I worked on food preservation projects. I was involved in civic endeavors. Even my own family's knocking on doors and stuffing of envelopes for favorite candidates was connected to my 4-H pursuits. I remember thinking that I didn't know what I would be good at but that I should take every opportunity to find out. I might learn a new skill. I might find out something important about myself. I should dive in! It was nearly a philosophy of life for me at the time.

In all of this and more I was required to keep detailed records about processes, plans, and procedures. This skill seeped into my bones, making me the inveterate record keeper I am to this day. It has seen me in good stead in all the roles I have played in my life. This all came from the requirements of 4-H and the way most of the disciplines urged on me at that time in my life were treated as preparation for my future.

Yet, of the many defining experiences of my early life, it was our family dinnertime conversations that most shaped me. It sounds simple but it was profound. My parents simply framed the world for me as they talked about life during our family meals. Not only were they intelligent, thoughtful, and well-read, but they were pretty fearless in what they would discuss. A newspaper headline or a happening in town might raise a topic. The facts would be explored. The relevant principles of human conduct would surface. Someone might argue a perspective without factual support. This would be kindly explained at a later time. Always my parents displayed common sense and wisdom. Always they were simple and gentle in helping me understand ideas and happenings slightly out of my reach. Always the discussion melded seamlessly once again into their God-centered, America-loving, character-driven view of reality. Even today I refer to those invaluable lessons.

———————

I certainly had not fully arrived as a conservative by the time I went off to college. Obviously, there was much more for me to learn. Yet the important truth of my early life is that conservatism entered my mind and heart through my environment. I acquired it organically, by living in the world my parents and Laurel, Mississippi, created for me. No one dictated. No one commanded. Instead, there were wise words and faithful examples and loving opportunities to observe and experience on my own.

It would be naïve of me to ever think that the whole world could ever be the world of my childhood. It would be silly to think that all parents might be like mine were. Yet surely I am not being too idealistic to hope for a world of strong families, of supportive community, of noble values, and of admirable goals. Surely I am not imposing my past on other people's futures to wish them a life with God in his heaven and parents often home and sterling values ever present and the constant message from all directions that every child can be whatever they have been destined to be.

Don't misunderstand. I live in the real world. I'm not trapped in some sentimental Instagram post. I'm a United States senator and I deal with some of the toughest human crises on earth. I understand the horrors millions face every day. Yet I believe we start to build a better world by envisioning one first. For me that vision is rooted in my life growing up in Laurel, Mississippi, surrounded by relatives, and I do not apologize for hoping that the same love, safety, guidance, and opportunity I was given might be the gift of every child on earth. This, I believe, is part of a conservative faith.

Chapter Three

How Destinies Turn

*O*pportunity. A positive word. A pleasant word. It resonates with a sense of possibility and promises yet unfilled. I like to think of opportunities as doors that are already open. Someone has seen you coming and made a way. All you have to do is step inside.

It would be nice to think that life is always this way, wouldn't it? Doors open. People welcoming. I think you know, though, it isn't. Most doors are closed. Few people are ever standing there waiting for you to arrive. The world can harshly send you the message over and over again that there is nothing for you here. Move on!

What should you do? Shrink back in bitterness? No. Bitterness is a cancer to the soul, a destiny killer. Don't take that path. Should you adjust your expectations, perhaps settle for less than you dreamed? No. Once you start downgrading your dreams, the downward slide never ends. Keep your dreams alive. Always.

What you should do is what I had to learn to do. Make your own opportunities. Open your own doors. Keep banging away until the obstacles give way.

Let me explain.

I went to college at Mississippi State University. I managed to pay for my first year with a national 4-H Club scholarship and some beauty pageant scholarships I had won. As I faced my last three years, I couldn't figure out how to make it work. I didn't want to take out loans. I also loved campus life and didn't want to do a work-study program. How would I earn the money to stay in school?

It occurred to me that my brother, James, who is two years older than I am, had worked at a great job selling books for the Southwestern Company. He had put in eighty hours a week on straight commission, but he had earned several thousand dollars the previous summer—and that was in early 1970s dollars! The job sounded perfect to me. You could work as hard and as long as you wanted to, become good at your job, and earn as much money as your abilities allowed. This was my kind of job! I decided to apply.

That was when I hit a huge obstacle. The Southwestern sales teams were all male. The company simply didn't recruit women. The door was closed.

I was devastated. Yet I had to admit that there was more than just bias to this policy. For many years I had watched as young men like my brother went out into the world during their college years and sold books for Southwestern. These intrepid souls would journey to untapped regions, make arrangements to stay in the back room of a sympathetic family's home, and begin selling Southwestern books door-to-door.

It was not a job for the faint of heart. Rejection came as did successes. Both had to be managed. Plans had to be made and executed. Records had to be kept. A salesman was always accountable to district managers and to the policies of the company. It wasn't for everyone, but those who stuck it out often had transforming experiences that served them well for the rest of their lives. They also earned the money they needed for school and to launch them into the next phase of their lives.

It all sounded wonderful to me, yet no female teams sold

for Southwestern. You can understand why. The company simply wasn't willing to send a girl out on her own to stay with families she barely knew and then ask her to knock on the doors of strangers all day, all far from home.

Now, I am a fairly determined person. I believe the passionate spirit that abides in me is one of my God-given gifts. When I set my mind to something, I don't give up—and I wanted to be a salesman for Southwestern. I knew I could do a good job. I wanted to prove myself, build an organization, and earn enough money for school. I wanted to rise. Frankly, I also wanted to pay my tuition and have the clothes, car, and freedom during the school year that every girl wants. It was time to create my own opportunity.

I convinced my brother to ask the company if they would make an exception and allow a woman to sell door-to-door. Naturally, there was the initial hesitation you would expect. There was much discussion and deferral and debate. There was also a great deal of pleading and case making on my part. Finally, though, James and I got his sales manager to agree to let me sell. I was beyond excited!

There were some stipulations, of course. Opportunities almost always come with stipulations. I would not be part of one of the men's sales teams. I would have to stay at home and sell only in Mississippi. I would also not have a student manager or a team to work with. I would need to handle my own hours, discipline myself, motivate myself, and make success happen—all on my own. The Southwestern folks couldn't have known how much of a fit this was for me. I was a self-starter, and nothing could have motivated me quite like putting me in a position to achieve through my own efforts—particularly if it meant proving myself to the boys!

I had my doubters. "You won't last two weeks," one friend taunted. I was feisty. "Wanna bet?" I responded. Let me cut to the chase and tell you that I collected on that debt.

In fact, I did not last just two weeks. I worked for Southwestern all through the rest of college and afterward. It was a magnificent training ground for me. When you sell door-to-door, you have to face your fears. You never know what is on the other side of each door you knock on. Then, you have to immediately establish rapport with a person you have probably just interrupted in the middle of a busy day. By the way, you have about fifteen seconds to do this. You have to colorfully describe your product, find the felt need of the customer, match book to person, and close the sale. It is all about the dance of the sale: the approach, the tone of your voice, reducing defenses, and finding out how to serve the customer whether they realize that's what you're doing or not. Thankfully, I proved pretty adept at all of this.

The story of my early sales experience was told in a February 4, 1972, article in the *Reflector*, the student newspaper of Mississippi State University. Entitled "Book Sellers End Sex Discrimination," the article declared that Southwestern had hired a person "with shoulder length hair," an indication of the short hairstyles for men at that time. The truth is, as the accompanying photo shows, I had big, bouncy, 1970s hair that was far beyond just shoulder length.

What makes me laugh all these years later is my recounting of how southern women would answer the door and say, "Sugar, how old are you? You don't look old enough to be out in the world!" Of course, I had to show my combative side by also telling the reporter, "People have been brainwashed. They think women aren't capable of that type of work. I wasn't going to quit. When things weren't too good I remembered that people shoved doors shut in…ladies' faces every day."[1] See, I was quite the radical for 1972!

Breaking the glass ceiling at Southwestern was important, but as important was the fact that I was being given opportunity to gain skills I might never have had at another company. My second summer with Southwestern I oversaw my own sales team. When I finished college, I capped off my Southwestern career by becoming a sales manager—truly stepping into the boys' club and changing the culture of the company. It was a school of hard knocks at times, but an invaluable school teaching invaluable lessons nevertheless.

What I learned from that first summer and the three summers afterward dug a well of wisdom and skill that I draw from every day. I had to build a team and keep each team member motivated. I had to mentor and coach. I learned that you manage things but you lead people. It isn't always easy. I had to develop sales and marketing skills. I had to craft reports that were better written than ever before. I taught myself how to ask the right questions to get the information I needed and how to maintain daily contact when I wanted to see improved performance. This was a challenge in a day before cell phones and email. And, yes, I had to overcome the biases and mistreatment that came from me being a woman.

I also had to grow up a bit and learn lessons about the dark side of human nature. Given my upbringing, I pretty much assumed everyone was going to tell me the truth. I quickly learned this wasn't always true. People faked sales numbers, lied about what they had done all day, and falsified every kind of report imaginable. Some were not beyond "borrowing" money or thinking that because they were good-looking or talented they could sidestep policies. Then there were those men who thought they could pull a fast one on a "little lady" if they just flirted a bit or hinted at improprieties.

The success I had that summer led to a stunning opportunity. Because female salespeople were a hot topic, the *New York Times* did an article that featured the Southwestern Company. Trust me, that's the last time the *New York Times* ever did me a favor! Still, a popular TV show at that time called *What's My Line?* contacted Southwestern to see if they had any females who might appear on the show. The program featured a panel that tried to figure out why that week's guest was exceptional or what their line of work was. The panel was even blindfolded during some episodes when the guest might otherwise be recognized. Well, I was a bit of an unexpected door-to-door salesman, and so whoever they talked to at Southwestern thought immediately of me.

In 1972, then, I ended up traveling to New York to appear on one of the most popular TV shows in the country. It was a blast! There I was, a little blond thing from Mississippi, trying to answer the panel's questions without giving too much away. It was a whole bunch of firsts rolled into one: my first time in New York, my first time on national television, and my first time being questioned before cameras about something worthwhile I had done.

Something else happened because of that show. A bookseller named Chuck, a University of Texas at Arlington student, happened to watch the program from his fraternity house near campus. He later said he decided right then and there that he had to meet this Marsha Wedgeworth and ask her for a date.

Now, part of the reason for his interest was that he had been the top salesman for Southwestern the previous year, and he was thrilled that one of the team made it onto national television. So, we met, appropriately, at sales school at Belmont College in Nashville. I remember thinking that this guy was Texas arrogant and awful, and that nothing between us would ever last. I must have changed my mind because I ended up marrying Chuck. We are still doing life together to this day!

Thank you, *New York Times*!

Thank you, *What's My Line?*!!

It was during the years I was a student at Mississippi State and was working for Southwestern that I came to a new understanding of the richness and depth of conservatism. The age in which I was living forced me toward this, I realize now. I went to college during the last tumultuous years of the Vietnam War. Richard Nixon was in the White House and Watergate filled the headlines. The U.S. Supreme Court ruled in the infamous *Roe v. Wade* abortion case, and the Senate passed the Equal Rights Amendment and sent it to the states for ratification. An economic recession was just then blanketing the nation, and baby boomers were also just then beginning to leave home or college and make their way in the world.

All of this was much observed and debated in my world. This gave me a chance to test my values against heated opposition and the attitudes of the times. At the MSU student union, a group of us gathered regularly to debate the issues of our day. We disagreed fiercely, but we were good friends, and this allowed us to learn from each other, to explore what we really believed, and to become more skilled in a contest of ideas. My most fiery opposition usually came from Marty Wiseman, the unceasing champion of liberalism. Oh, how we fought and raged and pleaded! It was wonderful. Marty and I are still good friends to this day—and I disagree with him just as much now as I ever have and always appreciate his friendship!

Though you may know where you came from and what you believe, it is important to listen to your critics, to hear truth from the mouth of your philosophical opponents. It sharpens you. It broadens you. It deepens your resolve for what you believe and it prepares you to state your case, no matter how large the stage. Always remember that our great nation and freedom's cause has been well served by robust, respectful political debate.

I knew as I stood on the MSU campus that I had come from a Republican family and a Republican town. I was also from a family of deep faith and a people of fiery patriotic and civic spirit. Yet as I confronted the wider world on that campus, I found my values deepening and not dissipating, as happens for some people. I became more certain of my beliefs and worldview, not through stubbornness but through the confirmation of great literature, wise professors, and my own dogged determination to chase down the truth.

Much of this confirmation came when I read *The Road to Serfdom* by Friedrich Hayek. It was like a Magna Carta of conservative economics for me. Hayek took western democracies to task for their centralized planning and totalitarianism. This socialist direction required restraint and servitude rather than equality and liberty, he argued. Instead, free markets were the best mechanism for humans to use for adjusting their activities toward each other because free markets do not require the arbitrary and artificial intrusion of authority. In other words, to put this in street language, we don't need government messing with our lives. We can use free markets and the ways of community life to create both prosperity and harmony.

Hayek's work introduced me to the broader world of the Austrian school of economics and through it to a thrilling philosophy of freedom that seemed increasingly challenged in the United States. I found this also when I read Ayn Rand's *Atlas Shrugged*, the story of productive people attempting to thrive in a socialist dystopia and then striking out to fashion a capitalist society based on reason and individualism. Not only was this book powerfully written but it also set in stark relief the two different views of man and government that seemed to be in play in the headlines of my college years.

I was also mentored by the works of Milton Friedman, particularly his *Capitalism and Freedom*, a classic. Though this book is indeed a learned work of economics, it seemed to me a celebration of the human spirit. Friedman argues that most of man's failures come from state programs and action, while most of man's genius has been unleashed through free markets and private pursuits. Friedman was a libertarian, which I am not, but his explanation of how centralism kills and freedom unleashes, how free markets liberate man's best and government domination squelches man's greatest abilities, changed me forever.

Now, I should be careful to say that most conservatives and all of these authors believe there are realms in which the legitimate authority of the state ought to be exercised. None of these folks are anarchists. Nor am I. Yet the most prosperous and peaceful societies exist when government is kept in its boundaries, when markets are free, when individuals can rise as high as their gifts and character carry them, when faith is protected, when the protections of police and the military are mighty and principled, and when a culture of enterprise and innovation is encouraged.

It has always been intriguing to me that the word *economics* literally means "house law." It is a word from ancient Greek that refers to the laws or principles for managing the finances of a home or family. I was particularly struck by this as I was reading the great works of conservatism in college and each summer while rising as a leader in Southwestern. My work in the company became the laboratory for me to test my conservative principles. I saw what strong leadership, individual creativity, and free markets could do to elevate people and produce wealth. I also saw what corruption produces, how fear shrinks the soul, how laziness ruins a life, how hard work nearly always wins the day, and how a good faith, free market exchange is a win-win moment that makes lives better and powers society forward.

I applied all of this to the public policy issues of the time. I am, for example, passionate about women and what they can achieve. Of course I believe that women ought to have the same rights as men, ought to be paid the same for the same work, and ought to be encouraged to break every glass ceiling that still exists. I should also say that though I love my southern heritage, I realize that women in the South often aren't given the same opportunities as men. I railed against this in my early years and I rail against this bigotry wherever it exists now.

Having said this, though, it is important for me also to say that I am on the record as opposed to the Equal Rights Amendment. Some folks are confused by this, yet my stance is simple and rational. I don't need new government actions and regulations to guarantee my rights as a woman. I already have them! The Constitution of the United States guarantees me the same freedoms and protections under the law as any other American citizen. I don't need an ERA. I don't need a paternal state. I don't need some new amendment to guarantee me what I already have as if I never had it. No, thank you. Just obey the Constitution, a genius document and gift to the American people, and all will be well. Any other claim is based in ignorance and creeping socialism. Plus, it leads one to believe that you don't have a right unless the government gives it to you!

This mirrors my early reasoning on dozens of other public policy issues. I thought of myself as in favor of the human spirit, human creativity, and human productivity. I understood private, nongovernmental groups as the engine of society—churches and businesses, clubs and associations. I believed that government that was as close to the people as possible—at the most local level—served the people best and was most accountable. The state and federal governments had their place, naturally, but being as huge and as distant from Main Street as they were, they could often get bloated, corrupt, and ineffective. I believed then, as I do now, in streamlined, limited, and smart government that had the role of protecting a free people rather than reducing them to servitude. With these pillars in place, a nation could thrive, its people could be all God intended them to be, and good from that nation might be sent out into the world.

This is who I was and what I believed as I finished my studies at MSU. My college experience had added scholarship to what I already believed. I saw a connection between dinnertime conversations at the Wedgeworth house and the writings of Austrian economists. I understood how what I learned about Jesus in church fed into the civic virtues I learned in Laurel and thus into the broader patriotism I felt for my nation and her role in the world. I saw the overlap between how my parents ran our family finances and how the nation ought to handle taxes and governmental spending and foreign aid and times of crisis. It all congealed during my college years; all became a seamless garment of conservatism that I loved and that I urged as widely as I could.

I certainly had not learned everything I needed to know about conservatism by the time I graduated from college. Yet I have always believed that learning is a process, one that is ongoing. Even now, I always try to discover something new every day, and I encourage my children to do the same. This has helped me to stay sharp in a variety of arenas. Naturally, I would come to understand policies and procedures, the mechanisms of how the world works and the ways of society that you must know to get things done. But the rock-solid, unbending values, the worldview, the unshakeable views of God, man, and government were all in place.

———————————

Chuck and I each worked with Southwestern after college, and that was how we ended up in Nashville. I give that company a lot of credit for lessons learned that have influenced my career. They gave a small-town southern girl a chance to rise. They took a risk on me. I hope I repaid that trust in full. Yet here is what I know: I would not be where I am now—a woman in the United States Senate—had I not been given a chance to face my fears, use my gifts, and reap rewards for my labors as part of a team out knocking on doors in the summer heat. Hear me shouting their praise and my gratitude from these pages. Hear me also shouting that the companies of America should open their doors and let women rise. Everyone will be the better for it.

I eventually went to work for the Castner Knott company,

a regional department store chain that operated throughout Tennessee, Alabama, and Kentucky. This placed me in relationship with one of the most important mentors I would ever have. His name was Ralph Glassford, Castner Knott's CEO. Though I was young for the role, I answered directly to Mr. Glassford while I ran the retail fashion and promotional events division of the company. He patiently taught me what I needed to know, was tolerant of my mistakes, and said he saw a spark of something exceptional in my work ethic that he wanted to encourage.

In return, I wanted to prove his assessment to be correct and gave this role my all. I put in play my gift for record keeping—thank you, 4-H Club!—and all the managerial skills I had acquired at Southwestern and all the skills I had developed leading campus organizations at MSU. What skills I didn't have, Mr. Glassford made sure I had a chance to learn. He taught me to keep my eye on results, on deliverables, and not to get distracted by the unnecessary things that tend to capture a busy executive's attention. Learning to prioritize tasks was one of the primary lessons I learned by watching and listening to him. It was also at Castner Knott that I gained respect for "flat," or horizontally organized, companies. We had a couple of store managers who fully believed in managing by "walking around." I saw that while vertical or more stratified organizations could cause executives to lose contact with the reality on the ground, flat organizations were close to the action, accountable, responsive, and lean.

After years of happily working with Castner Knott, I decided to start a consulting business of my own. Called Marketing Strategies, it was a sole proprietorship designed to help growing firms with their imaging. I loved this work and had deep experience in it by that time, and I also wanted the flexibility that came from running my own show. I had children. In addition, Chuck was busy traveling in his work, always in sales—first in the men's clothing industry and then in banking and financial services. For us, a stable house and home was at the top of our shared priority list, and we felt that giving me the opportunity to work from home and be a constant with our children was the option that best suited our family.

Though this could have been a quiet time for me, my mother's example of volunteerism stirred me to action. I look back now and realize that I was a civic whirlwind, from leading the Nashville Symphony Guild and Friends of Cheekwood to women's groups and nonprofit health care boards, church activities, and children's schools. These became family activities.

I could almost hear the family maxims sounding in my ears during this season. *Be productive. Give back to the community.*

Leave things better than you found them. I loved investing in my community, and I was also thankful that I could use my business skills and keep them sharp.

Always, I was involved in Republican Party happenings. Chuck and I gave a portion of our time to the Williamson County Young Republican organization. I loved it. I eventually became the chairman of the Republican Party in Williamson County. My main job was to get people to run for office. Believe me, in the 1990s, it wasn't easy. The kind of people you would want to run for public office were usually successful and happy to stay where they were. You had to prick their hearts, awaken a sense of calling and duty, and help them see how their unique gifts could make a difference in the important political battles of our time. In some sense, I felt like I had been doing this kind of work for years. It was sales. It was helping people see themselves and a product in a new light. It was closing the deal. I felt both at home and like I was working at a whole new level all at once.

In time, I became the candidate. My first was in 1992 and was a race for Al Gore's former congressional seat. The problem was that Al Gore was on a presidential ticket at that time, running as the vice presidential candidate alongside Bill Clinton. Al had huge visibility, which he wasn't averse to using to guarantee that his old congressional seat in Tennessee would continue to be held by a Democrat. I lost that race. So effective was Al's campaigning from his elevated platform that more people than ever voted in that election.

But I learned. How many times has that been said in history: "I lost, but I learned"? The next words are usually "And lived to fight on to victory another day!" That is what I did.

I went on to be the Middle Tennessee campaign chair for Governor Don Sundquist. I then led the Tennessee Film, Entertainment and Music Commission. Each role taught me invaluable lessons. Each prepared me for what was coming, though I could not have known it at the time. We live life looking forward into an unknown future. We have to trust that God sees the whole, that he is weaving his purposes in our lives. We only glimpse what has been woven when looking back. Only then do we get a perspective we could never have had all those years before. Until our true purposes are revealed, we have to trust, learn, prepare, and continue to pray that we will seek God's will for our lives.

I ran for the Tennessee state senate in 1998 and won. It was during my time in the state senate, which was from 1999 to 2003, that I led a massive effort to defeat a state income tax. We won, but there was blood on the ground when it was over.

When I say "massive," it is difficult to describe how intense and prolonged the fight was. As you would expect, the political establishment on both sides of the aisle favored the tax— "Grow government," they would say. "Everybody else has a tax; we should also." Of course, as a conservative who ran for office on a commitment to fight higher taxes and increased regulation, I strongly disagreed. I was the first to stand up and publicly oppose the tax plan. Therefore, I was on the tip of the spear and spent my entire time in the state senate pushing back against the pro-tax arguments, building a cadre of Tennesseans to stand up with me to defeat that tax. That fight will live in our state's history as a time when Tennesseans decided they wanted a more accountable, smaller government and were willing to make changes to achieve that goal. Tennessee is thriving economically today in large part because business and wealth is flooding into an income tax–free state. I'm grateful I played a role in this. I'm also grateful for the lessons learned.

Then in 2002, I ran successfully to serve in the U.S. House of Representatives from Tennessee's Seventh Congressional District. I served until 2019, which means I served during the presidencies of George W. Bush, Barack Obama, and Donald Trump. Then, in 2019, I became the first woman to serve in the United States Senate from the state of Tennessee, the role I occupy as I write these words.

Let's go back to the first paragraphs of this chapter. I was talking about opportunity. I was saying that sometimes you have to make your own opportunity. You have to open the doors for yourself when you find no one there to open them for you.

In the story of my professional life, the turning point came when I decided not to back off when Southwestern told me they didn't include women on their sales force. It was that moment, in my nineteenth year, when destiny turned for me. I might have taken their answer as final. I might have finished out my home and consumer economics degree at MSU, perhaps returned to Laurel or gone on to some other city, and lived a happy though perhaps less impacting life.

I might never have had the chance to learn all I have in business, never have served all the organizations I've been privileged to help shape. I might never have served in a state senate or helped to fight off an oppressive tax that would have prevented astonishing prosperity for my state. I also might not have entered the U.S. Senate or had the privilege to serve at the side of some of the finest of American presidents.

It all might have passed me by if I had not made my own opportunity. If I had not pushed open a door. If I had slunk back in bitterness or fear and lost vision, leaving me to a life that was a shadow of the one I was made for.

My point is not that Marsha Blackburn is some uniquely brave woman who did something no one else can do. It is quite the opposite. My point is that fortune favors the bold, that destinies turn in moments of courage, and that we often make our own opportunities as God gives us the power to act. This is the message of my life. This is the message I strive to model and that I call every American woman to live out—free of fear. "Mundane to magnificent" is a phrase I repeat to myself regularly to motivate myself to keep pushing when my load seems heavy. Indeed, many of the mundane tasks we do each day can be used to push open a door and pave a pathway to reach our goals.

Thank you, Hilman and Mary Jo Wedgeworth. Thank you, Laurel, Mississippi. Thank you, Southwestern. Thank you, Mr. Glassford and the Castner Knott team. And thank you, God, that you put divine fire in the human soul and then send us out boldly to fashion destinies under your guiding hand.

Chapter Four

A Five-Word Mission

H appy Warrior. If you want to know the words that live in my heart as I do my job in the U.S. Senate, there they are. I love what I do. I also find myself well suited for a good political battle, particularly when that battle is for something I believe in deeply. I see myself, feel myself, orient myself in terms of these words: Happy Warrior.

Some years ago, I challenged myself to take this a bit further. Yes, I fight, and yes, I'm happy in the fight, but what am I fighting for? I wasn't in any doubt about the answer to this question in my own mind, but I wanted to make it clearer for others. At the time, I was often asked what motivates me. Frankly, I found myself rambling a bit as I answered the question. It was because of my passion, but rambling is a politician's disease and I try to kill that disease whenever I detect it in my own speaking. I decided to crunch down my long-winded answer and create a simple elevator speech that would paint a picture of where my passions lay.

I hit on five words. They are my mission. They are my reason for nearly everything I do.

Faith.
Family.
Freedom.
Hope.
Opportunity.

Once I nailed these five, I started talking about them everywhere I went. In a sound-bite, tweet-length world, the brevity helped me. For longer speeches, I loved the chance to flesh out the five simple words that came straight from the heart and that came close to expressing my entire reason for being in the world. Every speech I was invited to give, wherever I had the chance, centered on these concepts.

I might have overdone it! I particularly wondered if this was true on one of my birthdays. I remember that I received a big beautiful box from my friends Darrell and Stevie Waltrip.

I'm sure you know that Darrell Waltrip is the NASCAR racing legend who was also a commentator for Fox Sports for many years. He owns a number of car dealerships around Franklin, Tennessee, and he and his wife, Stevie, have been dear friends of ours since we met in a Sunday school class decades ago.

When I opened the box they had given me, I found a Barbie-doll-pink racing suit. It was beautiful! Emblazoned on it were the names of my family members and patches of some of the military units I care deeply about. And right there in plain sight was my five-word mission statement: Faith. Family. Freedom. Hope. Opportunity. I know the Waltrips share these values, but I couldn't help wondering if when they thought of me they also thought of these words because I talk about them so much!

I guess it really doesn't matter, because I can't apologize anyway. I'm committed to them. Let me tell you one of the scenes from my life that makes me certain I am right to make these values my purpose.

In October 2003, I was part of an all-female congressional delegation to Iraq. Among the places we visited on that trip was a women's center in Mosul, not far from the headquarters of the 101st Airborne, where General David Petraeus was our host.

It was the women who captured me. You have to remember

what the women of Iraq had endured by that time. Their country had been scourged by war. Saddam and his sons had personally and vilely molested hundreds of women and created a culture of rape and sexual perversion throughout much of the Iraq they controlled. Kurdish women in particular had known gassings, starvation, torture, and unimaginable deprivation.

Now these women stood in a bombed-out shell of a building. They stared out of great, jagged holes in the walls that passed for windows. When they fixed their sad eyes on us—free women—from the United States, we could almost feel them scanning us for a semblance of hope, some sign that their lives could be better than they were.

I will never forget how they clung to our translated words. I remember in particular the way they ran their fingers over the raised letters on our business cards. I recall also the sweetness of the way they just wanted to stand near us. It was as though they were somehow fed by being in the presence of women from a land where there was freedom, a place where women had a chance to achieve. This was what they wanted. This was what they hoped for their children and their children's children. This hope, this promise, was what they wanted spilling out in their own land. Faith. Family. Freedom. Hope. Opportunity.

I realized something as I stood there with those amazing

Iraqi women. Instead of focusing exclusively on the concerns of today, women naturally think in terms of what will happen a year or twenty years in the future. Instead of focusing on the petty or the trivial, we focus on things that matter. What to wear to work or the fuss over the inconvenience of a flat tire pale in comparison to the thought of what grandchildren might one day have to endure. It is women who are often the guardians of these thoughts, these concerns. It is women who usually have the vision to call for a better world for their descendants. The mere thought of what could happen to their loved ones causes trivial concerns to fade away. Thank God.

FAITH

My invoking of God here leads us into my five words of mission, because God and my faith are at the heart of all that I am, all that I try to do as a U.S. senator. I believe we are made by a loving God. I believe this God has revealed his will for us and shown us the way he wants his creatures to live. I believe a similar faith in God was poured into the foundation of my country and that people faithful to God have worked hard through the centuries to assure that a vital faith continues to shape our national life.

This is why central to my life, and to the lives of many

conservative women, is a deep and abiding faith in God and in his will for America. It is this faith that allows me to stand resolute and firm as my value system is challenged, as it so often is today. In my opinion, protecting our right to exercise our faith is paramount to protecting our way of life. It is inconceivable to most of us that our nation would become one in which government controls the preaching of pastors or taxes churches or restricts the activities of ministries. Yet we face just such threats to religion in our nation today. This is shocking, particularly when being able to pray, being able to worship, being able to live out the dictates of our consciences without government intrusion are the rights our founders paid such a dear price to guarantee.

I know I can get very sentimental about this, but consider this one episode from our early history. In 1620, about a hundred people boarded a ship called the *Mayflower* in Southampton, England. One third of these people were children. One of the women in this group was pregnant. They sailed across the North Atlantic for sixty-six days. Think of it. Two months and six days of sailing in icy, surging seas. Because of the intense storms, this band of a hundred souls were often sealed in the "tween deck" for weeks at a time to keep them from being washed overboard. This meant every kind of human waste and expulsion would have been floating in inches-deep water on that deck. No privacy. No space of your own. Children crying. Sickness and disease plaguing everyone.

Why did they make that voyage? They told us in their journals and sermons. They made that voyage to the New World for the simple freedom to worship. That's the answer. They had been harried out of England for their faith. They had lived in libertine Holland for twelve years to the detriment of their faith. Finally their faith drove them to attempt a settlement in the New World, both to worship freely and to reach the natives with the message of God's love. It was all about their faith. It was all about securing a place to practice that faith freely.

This story and sacrifice are at the foundation of our nation, so you can understand, then, how furious it makes me when government dares to intrude upon the free exercise of religion in America today. It is why I believe that manning the borders of religious freedom in this country is nearly the same as standing guard for the nation itself, so thoroughly is faith in God woven into our national experience.

So, yes, faith is the first of my five words of mission. Yet my faith is not just a faith in God for the nation. It is also a very personal faith. I rely on God. I trust in his guidance. I know I can't do what I do without him. I think of this every time I'm at a town hall or the grocery store and someone grabs my arm to tell me they are praying for me. It means the world to me. And when they ask how they can best pray for me and for our nation, that's when I realize how much I rely on God. I'm tempted to give them an hour or two of prayer needs—not for me alone but for our country. I tell them to pray for our people. I ask them to pray that our leaders will seek wisdom and live lives grounded in faith. I ask them to pray for national protection and for evildoers to be caught and brought to justice and for corruption at every level to be exposed and judged. I always ask them to pray that God will lift our land to the heights of his purposes. I usually stop right there, but the fact that I could go on for hours causes me to realize how much I must have God in my life at every step.

FAMILY

It is in this matter of prayer that I most realize the value of the second word in my five-word mission and that is family. When I look at my prayer list, I always notice that it reflects the priorities of my life and this is why the name of every member of my family is at the top of the list. I'll tell you frankly that I would not want to live a day without them. The love of a parent for a child, the love of those precious grandchildren, is at times indescribable. What we share together feels like the very meaning of life.

My usual sign-off with my fabulous grandsons is this: "I love you more than life." These aren't just sweet words from their Marshie. I mean it with everything in me. One day Chase asked me what I meant by these words I say to him so often. I told him, "It means that I will give my life to save yours." I'll never forget the look on his little face as he pondered what that meant.

I cannot think about how much I love and rely on my family today without recalling all of the family members who have graced my life in years past. Those relationships were life changing and seem still to radiate their meaning from my core nearly every day. I miss them horribly—my dad and my grandparents, the uncles and aunts who helped to weave my life into what it is in the precious hours I spent with them. There is no family like a big, close, southern family, and it is not going too far to say that I was made into what God intended by family members who invested, sacrificed, and loved fiercely.

I have to explain what I mean by "southern family." If you are picturing a few people at dinner or going off to church together, you have only a small part of the story in your mind. Instead, picture a great crowd of people. Imagine a house filled to overflowing with cousins, aunts, uncles, grandparents, and a few friends from the neighborhood besides. A big, wide porch filled with all the overflow the house can't hold. Hear it in your imagination. Hear the screams of delight and the babies wanting attention and three kids asking three different mothers for some kind of permission and women in the kitchen and men talking shop. Smell the food and the perfume and maybe the scent of a fire on a chilly fall day. Then picture some of us working the grandparents' garden or picking berries or pecans or weeding the bed of prize-winning chrysanthemums. This was often the scene as I grew up. Even when we weren't all together this was still the spirit and the belonging that filled my life.

There was more than just the joy of being together that shaped us. A family as close as ours brought accountability. Once you understood who you were and who you belonged to, you didn't want to let anyone down. When you thought of doing something you knew you shouldn't do, you also started picturing the faces of those you would disappoint. You could envision the confrontation that would occur and how it would feel in the house for hours after. Okay, let me tell the truth! You also pictured the whooping that would land on you if you misbehaved! In other words, you were part of a people. You were committed to something. There were expectations. If you violated these expectations, you paid a price that was dear. All of these kept you—mainly—on the straight and narrow. They also kept you grateful for the people God had given you.

When Chuck and I started our own family, and when my siblings started into that same season, we carried what we had known into the next generation. We were not isolated islands. We loved each other, cared for each other, and nurtured each other.

It was as part of this desire to nurture that I began the practice of preparing lunch after church. Chuck and I routinely go to early church services on Sundays. Most everyone else in our family goes to later services. This gives me a chance to get ready because you can be sure that as soon as the benediction is given in that later service, the cars of everyone in my family are going to be heading to our house for a time of family fellowship, sharing—and food! I work to make it special and we have begun rituals that deepen the experience. Achievements are celebrated. If it is your birthday, you get to sit in the "King Chair." We are pretty much over the top about holidays. All of it makes memories. All of it binds us ever closer together.

I have learned that family keeps you grounded. It keeps you sensible and levelheaded. Family is the reason you wake up in the morning, work hard, and then get home as quickly as possible. Some people even leave good jobs and find new careers simply in order to spend more time with family. I've known people to uproot and move clear across the country to be near family. In my case, family is the reason I take that predawn flight to get to a meeting and then fly home on that last late-night flight, all to be back in time to drive the kids to school the next morning. Family is also the reason I make sure, no matter what is happening in Washington, that I am home for that beloved tradition of Sunday lunch every single week.

Family is not only at the center of my heart; it is also at the center of my reason for public service. The disturbing fact is that family life is under attack in America. I'm not being alarmist. I'm speaking the truth. There have been few times in American history when we have seen such vicious attacks on the institution of the family as we are experiencing today. Parents find themselves pushed aside by local school boards when it comes to decisions about what their children will learn. It is one reason why many families today choose to homeschool. Families also have to expose nearly every detail of their financial lives to get a college loan. Family-owned businesses are nearly drowning today in layers of regulations and contracts, many made necessary by our highly litigious society and the legal tactics of the political left in this country. And then, of course, there is abortion, the ultimate attack on family life. The fact that hundreds of babies in the womb are killed every day in this country tells us much about the state of motherhood and the state of the family in America today.

Given my role in Washington, I'm concerned about attacks on the family that might not occur to some other Americans. Just think, for example, about how adversely liberal tax policies affect families. These policies take a family's hard-earned tax dollars and send them straight to the federal government every month. Yet these families have almost no say in the matter. The government takes its cut first, and that cut is huge, usually amounting to a third or more of the average family's income. This may mean that Mom or Dad works a second job or that both parents have to work, pressured by mounting tax bills. Many families do without the things they need or want, simply to pay for a bloated federal budget. There is less free time to spend with children or with older relatives. There is less time for the meaningful life that government is supposed to protect, not compete with.

In increasing numbers of American households, tax policy has become the driver of the family budget. Research by the National Taxpayers Union shows that many times taxes are the largest single item in the family budget. America's families are stunned to find that this is true. They are horrified to see that their taxes are larger than their car payment. Of course, many forms of taxation impact them: income taxes, sales taxes, utility taxes. Americans are paying taxes from sunup to sundown. Put another way, the average American works for four and a half months of every year just to pay taxes. This is not the way it was meant to be.

Then, of course, there are also the burdens and barriers our courts put in the way of family. Think of the long list of decisions courts make that affect the family. They determine how much control parents have over their children, how a family's health care will be decided, how much religious preference each American family will be allowed, and a host of other decisions that can have the impact of weakening, shrinking, and even destroying our nation's families. Given the activism of liberal judiciary appointees, those of us who champion the family have to battle against judges who think they can legislate from the bench. Often their rulings destroy the most important connective tissue of our entire society—the family.

So you understand, then, why the word *family* is part of my five-word mission statement. I know the power of the noble family. I was produced by one. I understand what family has meant in American history. I am not deceived about the battle we are fighting for the family today. And, of course it is all personal for me. I do love my own family so much that I would, if necessary, give my life for each of them. I know many Americans feel just the same

FREEDOM

I remember a headline that grabbed me when I first saw it. It declared, "Freedom Stages a Comeback!" I had to ask: "A comeback?" I never knew freedom was out of style. I quickly read the article beneath that headline. It was a summary of how despotic regimes around the globe are facing protests and angry citizens clamoring for freedom. The people in these protesting throngs want to be free to live, to dream, to achieve. Finally, they are pushing back against the despotism that has held them in bondage. As I read this article, I thought again about how this kind of yearning for freedom is at the heart of the American dream.

In fact, it is nearly impossible to understand America without understanding the basic human drive for freedom. It was freedom that moved the Pilgrims to say their good-byes to family and friends they would never see again and board that leaky ship in hope of landing on a distant shore where they could live as they wished and dream of freer days yet to come. They were drawn by freedom, inspired by freedom, and powered by the hope of freedom to build a life in the New World. Much later in history, one of my heroes, Sojourner Truth, raised the banner of freedom for those who were ensnared by the evil of slavery. It was the hope of new freedom that moved many of our ancestors to journey to America, to steam past the Statue of Liberty in New York Harbor with tears in their eyes. And it was to restore freedom that many of our fathers and grandfathers fought in wars on foreign soil. In short, it is freedom that has powered the best of American history, and this is likely why the cry of freedom in the movie *Braveheart*, the lyrics of pop, rock, and soul music, the strains of our national anthem, and a thousand other declarations of freedom still move us to this day. It is what unites us. It is what gives our national experience meaning.

Like most women, I can't imagine the horror of living life in a society that didn't allow me to seek an education, worship as I please, love my spouse and family, vote, travel, or express my opinions. I find it hard to even conceive of living in fear of retribution from the government. It is impossible for me to picture my children and grandchildren facing a time when they experience a loss of freedom.

I can say all of this because I am an American. I live in a land of freedom, am possessed of a vision for freedom, and work nearly every day in Washington to make sure that our freedoms stand firm. I know there is still much work to do. There are conspiracies working in American politics and society to severely limit our freedoms and to put us in the clasp of leftist control. I stand against such incursions. I stand against the encroaching bondage of misguided liberalism. I hear a Braveheart-like cry of freedom in my soul as I serve my nation, and I pray my legacy might be greater freedom and self-determination for all Americans. Never far from my mind is Ronald Reagan's warning that American freedoms are always only a generation away from being lost.

HOPE

We often use the word *hope* half-heartedly. If someone asks us, say, if we are good at a certain skill, we might answer, "Well, I hope I am." It means we are unsure. It means we don't want to assert ourselves. We can't decide, and so we "hope."

Well, hope is much more than that! Hope is a claim on the future. Hope is an inner certainty of an outer condition that is yet unfulfilled. Hope is a driving of a stake, a planting of a flag, a declaration of intent about a day that has not yet arrived. Hope is believing in good things yet unseen.

This type of hope becomes a kind of fuel. It becomes a power for making things happen. It becomes the energy that allows us to align our work each day with the future we hope for. In other words, hope is not just an idle dream. It is the dynamo that makes dreams a reality.

And what do we hope? We likely carry the same kind of

hope that has filled American hearts for centuries. We hope for better days, a peaceful future, and a good life for future genera- tions. We hope our families will be healthy and prosperous. We hope our children will be wise and fruitful.

Yet hope goes beyond even this. As a legislator, I can tell you that many times hope shapes my decisions and my vote. I often have to choose between policies of hope and policies of fear. I frequently have to decide what kind of America I'm willing to go to battle for—one riddled with debilitating fear or one that rewards hope and the sacrifices of the hopeful. More times than I want to admit, I have looked at my colleagues in the House or the Senate and realized that many of them are making decisions rooted in fear—fear of losing an election, fear of a program not living up to its potential, fear of failure, and, more sordidly, fear of a bad headline.

I bet on hope every time. I believe that if you give Ameri- cans a shot at something, they will take it. If you give them a level playing field, they will succeed. Hope is a North Star for my life just as it is for my politics.

OPPORTUNITY

I have a friend who is a naturalized citizen of the United States. She often speaks of having won the lottery. What does she mean? She means that America is such a land of opportunity, such a place where every good and noble aspiration is possible, that she feels herself uniquely blessed as though she alone among millions won the lottery.

I often think about her as I travel the world and hear people speak of their view of America. There are hundreds of millions of people who look longingly to our shores and who would give all they have for a chance to live out the opportunities the average American takes for granted. Our country certainly is not perfect but it is perhaps the highest on the opportunity scale among the nations of the earth. It touches me to think of how many in the world dream of even having a chance to begin building their own version of the American dream.

Yet I want to tell you how I think of this idea of opportunity. Truthfully, opportunity in our nation means opportunity for me—and you—to make our own opportunities. It means having a chance to take a chance, finding a door cracked open and pushing boldly through that opening, or maximizing a slight possibility that graces our lives. I think of this as enlarging a narrow opening, stepping onto a pathway that is unknown but that might lead on to fortune. Perhaps if we are bold we might be able to lead a nonprofit organization to help others, or follow up a promising lead for a client, or make the most of a media opportunity. Whatever the slight crack in the door of destiny might be, we must live in the knowledge that opportunities are not completed victories that are handed to us. They are moments in which, if we defy our fear, we are allowed to take a first step on to greater things.

This understanding of opportunity makes me grateful, makes me a hard worker, and makes me eager to make as many opportunities for others as possible. It also makes me grateful for our ancestors in this country. They did not sail to shores with comforts awaiting them, with wealth already amassed. They sailed for months at a time and then often had to scratch out a meager existence in order to survive. We might be tempted to call this a failure. They saw it as an opportunity, just the slightest opening of possibilities that they could maximize through faith, courage, and labor. I love that my nation was built on such opportunities, and I'm devoted to seeing America be that kind of land of opportunity as long as I live.

These, then, are the five words that make me a Happy Warrior. They are the words tattooed on my heart, that frame my vision for my country, and that condition everything I do in politics. They are deeply personal to me while at the same time being as public as I can make them, but always they are the fire in my bones. Though it wouldn't be appropriate for me to wear that racing suit the Waltrips gave me years ago while I work—imagine me in a pink racing suit up on Capitol Hill!— I do wear these terms as my crest, my banner, and my marching orders.

I'm sure you can relate. In fact, I know a rising army of conservative women can relate—and I'm eager for them to make this nation in their image!

Chapter Five

A Noble Heritage

I am a humble conservative woman. I know I have said this before in this book. I'm likely to say it again. I love what conservatism stands for. I love its body of ideas. I love its history and what it seeks to do in the modern world. I am unreservedly devoted to that body of ideas. I am, I say again, honored to be called a conservative woman.

Yet if the only conservatism I knew was the kind that is portrayed in the media today, I would put as much distance between it and me as possible. That portrayal is a caricature, a cynical, disgusting cartoon. It's a straw man, really, purely a creation of the liberal imagination used to distract from the powerful, vibrant thing conservatism really is.

The left in this country wants people to think that conservatism is a coterie of old white men conspiring together to keep control of their ill-gotten power. If these men had their way, according to liberal fantasies, women would be unable to vote or hold a position much higher than chair of the Flower Arranging Committee at a church. African Americans would all be subservient and Hispanics would all be working in the fields—if they were allowed in the country at all. Asians would all be—well, in Asia. There would be no Muslims, few folks of any religion from the Middle East, and as few Canadians as possible. We would also do what we could to discourage the French.

That's not all. In their leftist fantasy, under conservatives the top 1 percent would own 80 percent of the country, and upward mobility for the rest would be a matter of moving from the fields to the factory. The military would be so advanced it would look like a scene from *Star Wars* and be so expensive it would nearly impoverish the nation. It would also be devoted to invading nearly every country on earth. Education would be too expensive for all but the few, home ownership would be happily enjoyed only by that small club at the top, and the rest would live in a world that looks like the scenes from *It's a Wonderful Life* after the character portrayed by Jimmy Stewart ceases to exist. In short, life for most people would be, in Thomas Hobbes's famous phrase, "solitary, poor, nasty, brutish, and short."

Of course, none of this is remotely true, but raising fears that it is true sure keeps liberal commentators employed and donations to liberal political campaigns pouring in.

The truth is that conservatism is a body of time-tested ideas that have come down to us through the centuries and that have proven themselves again and again. It is the counsel of the ages and it serves us best today by challenging the trendy and the avant-garde. It calls us to tradition. It calls us to wisdom. It calls us to freedom and to justice. It also reminds us that rapid social change is destabilizing, particularly when that change is engineered by the untethered, unhinged, and unimaginative global left.

Allow me, then, to tell you a bit about the glorious heritage of conservativism. If you are a conservative mainly because of where you stand in the current battles in American politics, it is important for you to also know where the ideas you love came from. If you are newly arrived to the conservative fold, I want you to know that you are finding a home in more than just a political movement. You have become part of a philosophy, a way of viewing life, that is based on eternal truths and the best wisdom of mankind, on just practices and a vision of unending freedom.

I also want you to know what you believe so you can help me do a little butt kicking when the political left comes looking for a fight! This book is called *The Mind of a Conservative Woman*, after all. Perhaps I should subtitle it *A Guide for Doing Intellectual Combat with American Liberals*!

But first, a word about idiots. The Greek word for *idiots* means "unlearned ones," and oh, do we have unlearned ones in the conservative ranks. Always have, always will. We also have knuckleheads, jerks, halfwits, cretins, simpletons, and jackasses. Every movement does.

Your job, though, is to make decisions about what you believe based on what certain ideas mean for your nation, for real human beings, and for the generations that come after you. Don't decide based on who is likable or witty. Don't decide based on hairstyles, makeup, and clothes. Please don't decide based on who looks cooler on *Oprah* or at the Grammys. Style cannot be a determining factor. I hear rumors in Washington that liberals give better cocktail parties than conservatives. Might be true. I don't know because I'm not invited to liberal cocktail parties. Still, I'm willing to concede. What I don't concede is that we conservatives must bow to any other political movement when it comes to wisdom, genius ideas, and policies that lead to national strength, prosperity, and freedom.

So if you are considering coming over to the conservative ranks, don't let our few outliers and nitwits keep you at bay. To paraphrase Jesus, we have Neanderthals and nitwits always with us. What you are looking for is an approach to public life that allows you to be the best you are made to be and affords the same opportunity to everyone else in our nation. In my opinion, you've found it.

––––––––––––

There are many ways to look at conservatism, and this is not because it is an unclear or uncertain body of ideas. It is because conservatism is like a magnificent diamond. A diamond is a single thing that reveals great beauty in every facet, from every angle, and in every variation of light. There are many ways to view it and to admire it. It is the same with conservatism, and each facet helps us understand this view of life and governance and also to explain it to the unconverted.

One of my husband's all-time favorite writers whom I have grown to love is William F. Buckley. I have always loved the stunningly simple definition of conservatism that he offered us in his splendid book, *Up from Liberalism*. In just twenty-one words, he captured nearly the entire DNA of conservative thought and life, revealing its alternative stance to much that defines the modern world. He said that the conservative worldview is based on "freedom, individuality, the sense of community, the sanctity of the family, the supremacy of the conscience, the spiritual view of life." I recommend you memorize these words. This is the best summation of our first principles I've ever heard and part of the phrasing that prompted me to develop my Big Five: faith, family, freedom, hope, and opportunity.

While we are talking about schemes of understanding conservatism that are easy to understand and easy to remember, allow me to describe the Five Cities Approach, as laid out for us by the brilliant Russell Kirk throughout his book *The Roots of an American Order*. Okay, grab a cup of coffee and get ready for a mental road trip. In this view, our vision for "ordered liberty," as some folks call conservatism, was begun thousands of years ago among the ancient Hebrews and the early Christians. While the rest of the world was mired in dictatorial paganism in which a king or tyrannical monarch ruled every aspect of human life, our early Hebrew and Christian forebears gave the world a different way. We'll call this the gift of Jerusalem.

These Hebrew ancestors taught that there is a God who is higher than kings, higher than the systems of men. This God created men and gave them purpose. This is important. Each human being, according to this view, has a divinely ordained purpose, a destiny, which ought to be honored and which earthly governments should ensure can be achieved unhindered. This same God established a moral order, the behavioral boundaries by which men and governments ought to conduct themselves.

The Hebrews also gave us, however unintentionally, the idea of federalism. When we read about their ancient history, we learn of twelve tribes that each had their own local governments but then joined together for specific purposes like defense, legal rulings, and worship. They were both one and many, both a unity and a diversity. Our founding fathers spoke of this Hebrew example often and built it into our American system. They gave us a federal government which had certain delegated purposes, defined by a Constitution and agreed to by the more powerful states.

Boy, those were the days, weren't they!

By the way, the word *federal* comes from the Latin word *foedus*, which means "compact" or "covenant." This helps us understand that our federal government is a government formed by a covenant or constitution. It is our "covenanted government," a covenant created through an agreement of the states.

The Christian aspect of that ancient part of our heritage gave us the idea of each ethnicity, each gender, and both rich and poor being equally created, equally chosen, and equally loved by God. We also received a distinct understanding of government from Paul's famous words in Romans 13. We learn from this that governments are ordained by God, a truth repeated in our Declaration of Independence and from many other public statements made by our founding fathers at the beginning of our republic.

Our early Christian parents then gave us an example of serving society. In a Roman Empire that persecuted them, the founding generations of the Christian church cared for the discarded, provided just courts, worked to abolish horrific practices like the gladiatorial games, and generally sought to meet the needs of a brutal and often callous Roman Empire.

By the way, before I leave the contributions of Jerusalem, I should say that I'm particularly grateful for the legacy of our Hebrew and Christian fathers and mothers because they laid the foundations for the ascent of women. This may come as a surprise to you, since our Judeo-Christian heritage is often blamed for the enslavement of women. Not true.

In the Bible I read, women are sometimes prophets. See the mention of Huldah in 2 Chronicles 34:22–29 and of Philip's daughters in Acts 21:9. Deborah was a judge and the story of Esther is about a queen who saved her nation. Women ministered with the apostle Paul and were "esteemed among the apostles." See Romans 16:3–4 and Romans 16:6. This is, of course, after women traveled with Jesus and supported him out of their own wealth. See Luke 8:1–3. And all of this is wrapped in the words of Paul in Galatians 3:26–28 that "in Christ" there is no "male or female." I'll leave theologians to dig out exactly what this means, but to my simple way of thinking, we should take it to mean exactly what it says!

This reminds me, by the way, of one of my favorite cartoons. A large group of men, obviously the early Christian apostles, are looking at a few women from the same period. They say to these women, "So ladies, thanks for being the first to witness and report the resurrection. We'll take it from here." It's funny, I know, but hopefully it is also a thought that will fester and cause some of the men around us to think twice before they speak.

So Jerusalem gave us a rich heritage. Athens is next. Our Greek forebears gave us deep roots in philosophy and in political self-awareness. If you read the American founding fathers and pay attention in turn to what they were reading, you'll find that they were constantly poring over Plato's *Republic*, the works of Aristotle, and the histories of Herodotus and Thucydides.

They also devoted themselves to the legacy of Rome, with its steely laws and social awareness. To read even small portions of our founders is to hear about Plutarch, Livy, and Tacitus. The word "Caesar" comes up constantly in debates and documents. And hardly anyone from the ancient world is referred to quite as much as Cicero, the Roman lawyer, statesman, and philosopher. Later generations honored the heritage given us by the Greeks and the Romans in the spectacular architecture you see in Washington, DC. Why are our national buildings and monuments adorned with Greek columns, Roman domes, and images of figures in togas standing in the Forum? It is to say that we are heirs of a body of ideas, millennia old and priceless. Let us declare these ideas in our national architecture, as well as in our philosophy of governing, forever.

This is the foundation of conservatism. As one leading conservative scholar wrote of this era, our conservative roots are found in Athens and Rome intertwined with "the Christian understanding of human duties and human hopes, of man redeemed."[1] All of these flowed through the medieval period, adding to this great legacy cherished customs, a devotion to learning, and an enduring system of valor.

On the foundation of Jerusalem, Athens, and Rome were built the contributions of London and Philadelphia. London gave us the British Parliament, which is often called the "Mother of Parliaments," and, of course, Philadelphia is the birthplace of the American Declaration of Independence and our U.S. Constitution. These are perhaps the world's greatest declarations that governments ought to be about preserving freedom and then explaining a great deal of how to do it.

Five cities. Five sources of heritage. Five pillars of a philosophy of the world and government. Conservatives today should seek to walk in the counsel of it all.

So we have William Buckley's twenty-one-word mini definition of conservatism as well as the helpful Five Cities Approach. Let's turn the diamond and look at another facet. One of the founding fathers of conservatism in America, Russell Kirk, offered a brief list of conservative principles that has served us well in explaining and defending the vision of our political faith. Let me break them out here as a way of offering another means of understanding the power, breadth, and brilliance of conservatism.

Kirk's first principle is "The conservative believes that there exists an enduring moral order." This may be the core belief that most distinguishes conservativism from other schools of political thought. We believe in a "transcendent order." That's fancy scholar language for the fact that we believe more exists than we can see. There is a God. There is revealed truth—not situational ethics, but the truth. As a result, there are moral absolutes and both our lives and our politics ought to conform to them.

Kirk stated this principle beautifully when he applied it to our times. He said that "the ruin of great nations in our century shows us the pit into which fall societies that mistake clever self-interest, or ingenious social controls, for pleasing alternatives to an oldfangled moral order."[2]

There are moral truths that nations ignore at their peril. There are absolutes that we violate to our destruction. I would suggest, for example, that if a nation does not honor human life and instead violently discards hundreds of babies every day—54 million in the United States since the *Roe v. Wade* ruling of 1973—that nation is in decline and risking the retribution that comes from violating the moral order that governs all of life. I would suggest the same of a nation that funds immorality with its tax dollars or that persecutes the free worship of God or that oppresses the weak and the poor who are near to God's heart.

Conservatives begin not with trendy ideas and the mandates of bureaucrats. Instead, they begin with the higher truth that there is a God and he has shown us the way to live. Therefore, his will ought to be observed in all our affairs. It is the way of wisdom. It is the way of peace. It is the way that we ensure one of the mottos of the American people, a motto we see on every dollar bill in our country: *Annuit Coeptis*—"God favors our undertakings."

The Marsha Blackburn version of this truth? *There's right. There's wrong. Pay attention to the difference in all you do.*

The second maxim from Russell Kirk is "The conservative adheres to custom, convention, and continuity." It has become fashionable to reject the wisdom handed down from previous generations, to think that we know better today than those who came before us. Yet there is a reason that some customs and conventions survive the centuries and are passed down to us. They are true. They work. They have been tested and proven, their genius revealed. A conservative takes this seriously and prefers the truths handed down to us from ages past over the thin theories coming today from a university political science department tenured professor or the chanted demands of an enraged mob.

Kirk had a wicked sense of humor as well as a grasp on the spirituality of conservatism. Both are revealed in this beautiful explanation of continuity: "Conservatives are champions of custom, convention, and continuity because they prefer the devil they know to the devil they don't know. Order and justice and freedom, they believe, are the artificial products of a long social experience, the result of centuries of trial and reflection and sacrifice. Thus the body social is a kind of spiritual corporation, comparable to the church; it may even be called a community of souls."[3]

This is how I see government and my role in it. I certainly

want change where it is needed. I'm even willing to help bring about radical change where the situations demand. Yet I always stop to consider the wisdom of the ancients. I always pause to keep in mind that rapid social change is often destabilizing and even destructive.

Modern liberals are always talking about a revolution of this and a revolution of that. Kirk's principle reminds us that revolution is a cure that kills, that it "slices through the arteries of a culture."[4] In other words, be careful.

The Marsha Blackburn version? *Listen to the past. It will make the present better.*

The third Kirk truth is "Conservatives believe in what may be called the principle of prescription." This is an extension of the second principle. He meant by this, as he wrote, that "conservatives sense that modern men and women are dwarfs on the shoulders of giants, able to see farther than their ancestors only because of the great stature of those who have preceded us in time."[5] We believe, then, in the wisdom of our ancestors, in the ponderings of the ancients, and in things established by "immemorial usage." This includes morals but goes beyond it.

I'm the first to concede that our forebears were just plain wrong about some matters. Keep in mind that I'm a woman and that people of my gender did not get the right to vote in this country until the Nineteenth Amendment was ratified in 1920. I certainly consider the sidelining of women in our nation's history to be a massive blind spot on the part of our ancestors. No one is claiming that the past was perfect or that all who came before us were without defect. We don't seek to rewrite the past—we learn from it.

Still, we are fools to think all wisdom originates with us. Much folly and pain has been unleashed in recent history through what passes for innovation and originality when it comes to government. A wise man once said that "the individual is foolish, but the species is wise."[6] Isn't it smart to consider what the ancients had to say before we charge ahead based on ideas that just popped into our heads?

I want those who lead me to know the best thinking of humankind, to master what has come before, what is tested, what is agreed to, and what has worked. That's what I want my surgeon to do. It's what I want the pilot on my next flight to do. (Definitely it's what I want the cooks to do in the next restaurant I go to.) Do what is known to work! Don't just pull something out of your bag of magic tricks! Don't just make stuff up! Not when lives depend upon you and so much is at stake. This is how conservatives think about policy and governance. Let the ancients whisper in our ears as we decide the course of the nation. A little humility wouldn't hurt.

The Marsha Blackburn summary: *Some folks from the past were smarter than you are. Let them guide you. Learn from the past so you don't repeat those mistakes.*

The fourth of Russell Kirk's conservative building blocks is "Conservatives are guided by their principle of prudence." Plato taught us that prudence in a statesman is the chief of the virtues. It's true. In our day, we often move too quickly, too hurriedly, in public policy. A recent book, a crowdsourced idea, a pithy phrase can guide liberal thinking and lead the left to demand radical change almost overnight. I love the wisdom in John Randolph's famous words: "Providence moves slowly, but the devil always hurries."[7]

American society is complex, more so today than ever. You have to be careful. Not fearful, but careful. You can tinker with something in one part of our nation, thinking you are doing great good, only to find out that the law of unintended—and negative—consequences is doing great damage somewhere else. The solution is to consider long and only then to act quickly. If you think a process of study and pondering is taking too much time and you're eager to get to the action, just consider how much time can be lost in having to repair the damage from misguided policies. As Kirk said with a wink, "Sudden and slashing reforms are as perilous as sudden and slashing surgery."[8]

Marsha Blackburn's version: *Slow down when it comes to governing. Knee-jerk reactions usually end up having to be revisited. Take your time and do it right the first time.*

———————

The fifth genius truth of conservatism is "Conservatives pay attention to the principle of variety." We know that this is true, though we often don't apply it to governing. The fact is that human beings differ from each other. They have different gifts, different interests, different capabilities, and certainly different ideas and dreams. We humans are not robots. Nor were we created by an uncreative God. We vary. We are different types. Each one of us is unique. Diversity should be seen as a strength.

This means, of course, that there will naturally be inequalities, that we will all rise and achieve differently. While a society does not want to leave suffering untended, it also cannot ensure that all people have the same things or live the same lives. We can guarantee freedom and opportunity but not results.

Liberalism thinks in just the opposite way. To them, everyone is merely an economic unit. Every policy is one size fits
all. To the left, human beings are automatons that should be
impacted by government programs in exactly the same way
with exactly the same results. This is foolishness, and if we
insist upon everyone being exactly the same and responding
to government in absolute uniformity, then we make a society
that looks like the goose-stepping tyrannies that have blighted
history.

No, there is variety. There are differences. They should be
celebrated and understood as part of the beauty of life. As Kirk
said with his trademark wit, "The only true forms of equality
are equality at the Last Judgment and equality before a just
court of law; all other attempts at leveling must lead, at best, to
social stagnation."[9]

The Marsha Blackburn version? *You know people are crazy
different from each other. You've been to a family reunion, for
heaven's sake! Lead like you know it. Meet people where they are!*

The sixth Kirk principle is "Conservatives are chastened by
their principle of imperfectability." This is a Judeo-Christian
concept that liberals tend to ignore. Human beings are fallen.

They are flawed. There is no perfection in this life, and constantly insisting on the ideal, on utopia, in public policy will only result in silly programs and ethereal policies that have no anchor in the real world.

Conservatives are not cynical and hardened, but we do believe in the hard realities of life in this world. There is evil. There are screw-ups. There are failures. There are unintended consequences. So, we need locks. We need checks and balances, separation of powers, and other such mechanisms to check both pride and folly. We need wise police and a strong military and the best systems to keep people safe. We also need to plan for the fact that stuff goes wrong at times. To paraphrase what Robert Burns said in his poem "To a Mouse": "The best laid plans of mice and men often go awry."

No one summarizes this truth better than Russell Kirk himself: "The ideologues who promise the perfection of man and society have converted a great part of the twentieth-century world into a terrestrial hell." It is true. Think of Hitler. His attempts at exterminating the Jews were all launched in a misguided attempt to perfect the human race. Think of Stalin and his insane attempts at ideological purity. Think of any other tyranny of recent centuries. They sought to make things perfect. They tried to remove impurities, whatever the cost. Life could be perfect, they believed, if only the price for it would be paid. And the price was paid—in blood, in lives, in lost generations. Give me conservative policies rooted in the real world and a moral order any day. That is the way to an enduring freedom.

Marsha Blackburn's Tennessee version? *We are all human, no one is perfect, and we want a quick fix—some more than others. Let's keep this in mind as we try to run a country.*

The seventh maxim is "Conservatives are persuaded that freedom and property are closely linked." The acid test for freedom in any society is whether men and women are allowed to do pretty much as they wish with their property. Can they own property, sell property, acquire more property, and control their property as they choose so long as they do not hurt others? In short, keep your eye on guarantees of property rights. That's where the line of freedom lies.

Now, liberals want us to think that property rights are merely the claims of the wealthy trying to hang on to what they have. Wrong! Instead, it is property rights that are at the foundation of a people's ability to rise. In fact, it's at the foundation of the entire idea of the American dream. Yes, we are more than mere consumers and owners. We are spiritual, artistic, and intellectual beings as well. Yet if you don't have basic rights over your property, then how free to be spiritual, artistic, and intellectual are you going to be?

Liberal politics are all about confiscation. They are all about plunder. They do nothing but seek to take from one group and give to another, to deny rights to some in order for some weirdo kind of equality to be achieved. It never works. It is unjust. It is wrongheaded. Redistribution of wealth has never worked.

The solution, instead, is policies that allow all to own, all to trade, all to rise, and all to pass what they have acquired on to the next generation. Most programs of the bloated socialist state cut across property rights, destroy prosperity, and demolish incentive. I don't want to live in a liberal, socialist hell. I want to live where property and ownership are encouraged, protected, and, where possible, enhanced. That's the America I continue to dream of.

The Marsha Blackburn summary: *If you can't do what you want with what you own—as long as you don't hurt anybody—you aren't fully free. Wake up!*

The eighth Kirk principle is "Conservatives uphold voluntary community, quite as they oppose involuntary collectivism." A conservative believes that people should be free to live where they want and then bond with others in their community to make their lives better. This is Kirk's "voluntary community." It is what has made America great. Think of the contributions of neighborhood groups, churches, synagogues, mosques, local political bodies, organizations devoted to improvement of some area of life, and a hundred other types of clubs and private groups. They are voluntary. They are freely joined. They devote themselves to important causes and they make our lives better.

Yet when the functions of these groups are passed to a bloated federal government, the community suffers. There is no freedom. There is only demand and mandate and insistence under threat of law. We conservatives believe that the more voluntary, the more local, and the more privately funded a charity or a social organization is, the more effective it is. It will do greater good than any government could and it will also help create a culture of social improvement and generosity that will spread.

Remember Barack Obama's "Life of Julia"? Well, she lived in a world without voluntary organizations. She lived without community, without helping organizations that gave her belonging or opportunity or inspiration or a chance to do good in the world. Her main relationship was with the federal government, and that's why even liberals scoffed at Julia's sad, socialist existence. We are made for a better life. Free, voluntary, benevolent organizations can make that better life happen nationwide—and they are!

Marsha Blackburn's version? *Get government off my back, out of my pocketbook, and off my computer. We've got this and do not need the federal government's help!*

The ninth Kirk principle is "The conservative perceives the need for prudent restraints upon power and upon human passions." We've heard it many times. Lord Acton told us that "power tends to corrupt, and absolute power corrupts absolutely." He was right. Put power in the hands of fallen, flawed people and that power can often be abused. That's why we need restraints. We need barriers to domination and despotism.

We also need the wisdom of our founding fathers. When I read the writings of that founding generation of Americans, I'm always struck by their real-world suspicions of human nature. They were a visionary, optimistic people, but they did not trust rulers, the people, or even one another very much. They knew what could go wrong. They had lived under English tyranny. They wanted systems in place to ensure that no man's will would dominate, that no faction could gain control. That was why they gave us a federal government divided into three branches. They wanted these branches to keep one another on the straight and narrow path. It was why they gave us checks and balances and vetoes and judicial review and dozens of other mechanisms to check the dictatorial, conspiratorial impulse in human nature. It was all designed to keep us free and prosperous. It was worth the price. It has saved us time and again.

Senator Blackburn? *Some folks will try to take over the world if you let them. Do yourself a favor. Don't let them!*

Finally, Kirk told us, "The thinking conservative understands that permanence and change must be recognized and reconciled in a vigorous society." Read what he wrote in his classic work, *The Politics of Prudence*:

The Permanence of a society is formed by those enduring interests and convictions that gives us stability and continuity; without that Permanence, the fountains of the great deep are broken up, society slipping into anarchy. The Progression in a society is that spirit and that body of talents which urge us on to prudent reform and improvement; without that Progression, a people stagnate.[10]

This, again, shows the realistic way conservatives view the world. We don't expect a perfect world. We don't expect only good from the lives of human beings. We also don't think everything about a nation proceeds all on one course at the same time. Many things are happening most every moment, some upward and some downward. Some things are remaining the same and some are changing. It's what you want in a stable society. We need reforms and progress, but there are also things that should always remain the same. The constants are our moorings.

This is simply the way it is in all of life. You have a body. It changes. We all know that. But you also count on some things remaining the same. This is what makes us individuals. Think about it. You fall in love with someone and then live with them for years. They change, don't they? You want them to. You want them to grow and improve, and you even find it sweet when you both start to grow old together and show the signs of aging. Yet always you're looking into those same eyes you first fell in love with. Always that laugh is the same. Thank God.

Some things change, others stay the same. You wouldn't want it any other way.

It's the same with nations. We want some things about the United States to never change. I don't want our magnificent vistas, our inspiring monuments, and our bedrock traditions and laws to change much at all. There are also a thousand things I love about American life that I hope are as true for my great-grandchildren as they are for me. Yet right alongside this permanence has to be progress. We need it in arenas like technological innovation. We need a constantly improved military. We want to transform poverty into prosperity, defeat racism, radically improve education, figure out wise solutions for our immigration crisis, and make smart changes in a hundred other arenas.

What we don't do is try to change everything in the name of progress. This is folly, and it is the kind of folly that some folks on the left specialize in. If they were in control, they would make changes that feel like progress when in fact they would merely be destroying our age-old foundations in this blessed land. They would do this rather than make the more meaningful changes that are really needed. This is what the radical left in America has always done.

So the wise person realizes, as Kirk taught us, "that nothing in a society should ever be wholly old, and that nothing should ever be wholly new. This is the means of conservation of a nation, just as it is the means of conservation of a living organism."[11]

The Marsha Blackburn edition? *The more things try to change, the more they might need to stay the same. Or be careful what you wish for...*

So we've turned the diamond of conservatism with William Buckley, with the help of five cities through history, and with the guidance of Russell Kirk. We have yet to hear from some of the statesmen and writers who brought the counsel of the ages to bear on the founding era of our country. We don't know conservatism unless we hear their words, and we don't honor them as we should unless we give them a chapter of their own. Trust me. This will change you.

Chapter Six

A Noble Heritage —
For Women, Too!

Perhaps the greatest champion of conservatism in all of history was a man who stood between two revolutions. His name was Edmund Burke, and he stood between the American Revolution and the French Revolution, and the experience helped to make him a father of modern conservatism.

You likely know a good deal about the American Revolution, but we tend to know far less about the French Revolution. It is important that we know a bit, though, particularly if we are going to understand Burke. Let me describe just a bit of that horrible time in France. And because I want you to feel it as well as think it, I'm going to describe it almost like it is a scene in a Hollywood movie. This will increase its impact on you and also give you a greater love for Mr. Burke.

Come with me now. We are in the Cathedral of Notre Dame in Paris. It is late in the 1700s. On the streets, shouts of "Liberty!" sound loudly and often. The citizens of France are celebrating. They are convinced that a new age is about to dawn.

And it is true. A revolution is indeed underway. The old regime in France is falling and a new reign of the people, of reason, and of atheism is beginning.

It won't be pretty. Before it is over, tens of thousands will be beheaded by use of an ingenious new machine called the guillotine. Ten thousand more will die in prison. A princess will be raped and dismembered in the streets. In the city of Nantes, 1,800 will be drowned. The king's minister of finance will be beheaded and his head, stuffed with straw, will be paraded through the streets of Paris. A thousand men will lose their lives when a mob storms the Tuileries Palace. Some 1,200 people will die when another enraged mob fights its way to the Abbey de Saint-Germain-des-Pres, jumps the abbey's wall, and then kills 150 clergymen with pikes and axes.

Yet the leaders of this revolution are not concerned about violence. Shed blood will purify the land, they believe. Let it flow.

On this day, though, there is a coronation at the beloved Christian cathedral of Notre Dame. It marks the beginning of a new religion. Already the Christian calendar has been discarded in favor of a new one with a ten-day week. Already churches have been made state property, clergymen have been forced to swear allegiance to the French state, and Christian ethics have been reworked to fit the bawdiness of the times.

Picture this. We are in the huge crowd that is standing along the aisles of the grand cathedral. Dignitaries are assembled in all their finery. The ceremony begins. Music begins to rise. Suddenly, completely naked women begin gyrating down the aisles. There is much leaping and swirling, much revealing of bodies in an intentionally erotic display. Unable to contain themselves, some in attendance answer their lust with willing partners in the dark corners of the church, all while the procession moves by.

Trumpets sound above this commotion, and now a throne appears. It is held up by poles resting on the shoulders of well-muscled men. On this throne sits the Goddess of Liberty. This is what they call her. She is actually a well-endowed prostitute, who now displays her wares as part of the mocking tone of the whole affair. She is carried, accompanied by great fanfare, to the high altar of the church. This is usually used for serving communion. This is where the Bible normally rests. Now this same high altar bears the imprint of a prostitute's behind.

The crowd erupts into a hymn as the "Goddess" takes her place. It is the "Hymn to Liberty." Some in the crowd weep. The naked dancers now put on the robes usually worn by the priests and continue their seductive dances. Wheelbarrows of objects once used for Christian worship—censers, communion plates, crosses, and goblets—are offered in worship of the nation's new queen. There is much shouting and weeping and raucous celebration. There is much rebellion against what was once thought to be right and wrong. By the end of the day, all of Paris—and ultimately all of France—will be filled with the spirit of this near orgy at the Cathedral of Notre Dame.

The Revolution lives. The secular state is born. Reason reigns. Religion is dead. Long live the Revolution!

It is a troubling scene, isn't it? So much violence and excess. So much crudity and arrogance.

Yet if this brief description of a few moments in the French Revolution bothers us all these year later, imagine how much it must have bothered Edmund Burke. He was an English statesman, and he was horrified by what he saw in France. His response to it would help make him one of the greatest voices of conservatism the world has ever known. In fact, he is often described as creating modern conservative thought, the man who gave conservative ideas inspiring expression just as the United States was being created.

Burke was born in Dublin in 1729, the son of a lawyer father. He was raised an Anglican and educated at Trinity College. Like so many great minds of history, though, it was his private reading that most shaped him. He reveled in Shakespeare, Spenser, and Milton, adored ancient writers like Virgil, Cicero, Homer, and Juvenal.

He studied law but his literary ability brought him early fame. He wrote books on philosophy, focusing on ethereal topics like beauty and the limits of reason. He challenged the harsh rationalism of his day, the same rationalism that fed the French Revolution unfolding across the channel. His prose was beyond the droning manner of many writers at the time. This gave him wide popularity.

He moved to London, married the Catholic daughter of a physician, and became editor of *The Annual Register*, a publication that continues to this day. Publishing led him into politics. In 1765, he was appointed the private secretary of the prime minister. Eventually, he won a seat in the House of Commons.

It was the beginning of a career that lasted twenty-nine years. To the everlasting gratitude of us Americans, Burke served during the reign of King George III, which means he witnessed from within the British government the events leading to the American Revolution.

He became a supporter of the battle for freedom he saw unfolding in America and even defended the rights of the colonists in Parliament, risking the anger of the king. He saw the American cause as it really was—a conservative counter-revolution against an overreaching government. He loved the American vision of liberty, its wisdom for governing, its decentralized authority, its protection of commerce, and, as important, its commitment to upholding faith in God.

He was repelled by the French Revolution, though. The secularism, tyrannical state control, violence, and debauchery sickened him. He knew worship of reason would not last and that France at the time offered no laudable model to the nations of the world. He was a smart man who could see through the weak, dangerous ideas of the radicals in France. His writings about that revolution were nearly prophetic and help us today to recognize the threat of a controlling central government and what people lose when the state strips them of rights and responsibilities. They become slaves as surely as any people have ever been slaves.

We should try to understand the basics of Burke's philosophy, since it has shaped so much of our world. All that he did and thought was deeply rooted in his Christian faith. He once declared, "Religion is the basis of civil society, and the source of all good and of all comfort."[1] He believed strongly that the morals drawn from religion are the basis for making of laws.

This foundational belief shaped everything else about his thinking and his statesmanship. He believed as other political thinkers of his day, like Hobbes and Rousseau did, that "society is indeed a contract." Yet for Burke, that contract was not between rulers and the ruled, but between God and man. This was the foundation for government as well as all human conduct.

It is not hard to find the imprint of this idea on our American founding fathers. Listen again to the opening words of our Declaration of Independence. Hear the influence of Burke, and of our Hebrew and Christian forebears, in the words: "We hold these Truths to be self-evident, that all Men are created equal, that they are endowed by their Creator with certain unalienable Rights, that among these are Life, Liberty and the Pursuit of Happiness.—That to secure these Rights, Governments are instituted among Men."

Notice that according to our founding document, man is

made by God and granted rights by God. The role of government is to protect these God-given rights. In light of this vision, government is at its best when it serves God's purposes—protecting the God-given rights of God-created human beings. This is a far cry from the liberalism of today, which seems intent upon stripping individuals of their rights as rapidly as possible and all in a crazed effort to create an all-controlling state.

It was his understanding of God, government, and men that made Burke such a fierce critic of the French Revolution. He called it "metaphysical madness."[2] He feared that the upheaval in France "would rend Europe limb from limb until subdued by force and a master."[3] He was right about this, and it was why he was fiercely determined that Britain "would not share in France's folly and that the whole of the civilized world must be awakened."[4] We should be grateful. His passion to see Britain kept from a French fate caused him to champion a philosophy of freedom that is at the foundation of the conservatism we know in the United States today.

What Burke saw so clearly was the folly of putting the rights of the state above the rights of the individual. He hated all socialism, all communist ideas. He saw the tyranny it would bring. He said often and loudly that for the French revolutionaries, "the will, the wish, the want, the liberty, the toil, the blood of individuals is nothing. Individuality is left out of their scheme of government. The state is all in all."[5]

It was this devotion to the philosophy of freedom and utter disgust with the excesses of the French Revolution that gave Burke such courage as a statesman. In one of his most famous declarations, he spoke of the obligation of politicians to serve the people while not caving into the opinions of the people. It was something he did all his life. These words are an indictment of the types of politicians we see on the political left today in America, small souls always trying to figure out where the political winds are blowing so they can act like they are in the lead. The truth is they can't lead, but they won't follow. Burke saw the silliness of this. Speaking to the British people of what a member of Parliament ought to be, he wrote:

His own unbiased opinion, his mature judgment, his enlightened conscience, he ought not to sacrifice to you, or any set of men living. These he does not derive from your pleasure—no, nor from the law and the constitution. They are a trust from providence, for the abuse of which he is deeply answerable. Your representative owes you, not his industry only, but his judgment; and he betrays, instead of serving you, if he sacrifices it to your opinion.[6]

Sentiments like these made him a republican with a small *r*. He believed not in the rule of the mob as he had seen it in the French Revolution. Instead, he believed that the people ought to choose the wisest of society to represent them and then trust that they would serve to the best of their abilities. This was the thinking of our founding fathers, as well. They distrusted democracy, as they said often. Instead, they believed that there were those called to serve in high office. The people ought to recognize them, elect them, and then send them forth to do their jobs.

When I read Burke, I'm always struck by his clear-headed understanding of what a free society should be. While radicals in France tore that nation apart trying to escape order and duty, constantly screaming about an abstract theory of rights, Burke talked about "the real rights of man." He once wrote, "Whatever each man can separately do, without trespassing upon others, he has a right to do for himself, and he has right to a fair portion of all which society, with all its combinations of skill and force, can do in his favor." He saw more clearly than most men of his time that this would produce a natural inequality in society. It was the way of things: "All men have equal rights, but not to equal things."[7]

Burke lived in the real world. He saw the savagery that came from overthrowing tradition and morality. He saw the danger of overheated radical ideas about universal rights, total equality, the overthrow of authority, and what a revolution could produce. Burke was so far ahead of his time that sometimes it sounds as though he is writing about the liberalism of today. Listen to this complaint: "By this unprincipled facility of changing the state as often, and as much, and in as many ways, as there are floating fancies or fashions, the whole chain and continuity of the commonwealth would be broken. No one generation could link with another. Men would become little better than the flies of a summer."[8]

I am grateful to Edmund Burke. We all should be. At a time when the United States was beginning to take its place among the nations of the world, Burke articulated a vision of a just and free society that challenged the radicalism then rising in Europe. We had been close to France during our revolution. We might well have followed in her path. You may remember from history class that there were French agents urging our founding fathers in a French direction. Thinkers and writers like Edmund Burke helped keep us from that precipice.

He urged that governments draw authority from God and the rights he had given to men. Burke thought these rights were sacred and were far more important than any prerogative of the state. Among these rights he would have listed worship, ownership of private property, freedom to achieve according to ability, and freedom from an overly intrusive state. At heart his was a philosophy of liberty, and every conservative today who fights off the intrusions of liberalism upon individual liberty is a son or daughter of Edmund Burke. As Russell Kirk wrote, Burke's ideas "did more than establish islands in the sea of radical thought: they provided the defenses of conservatism, on a great scale, that still stand and are not liable to fall in our time."[9]

What Burke taught, Alexis de Tocqueville had the privilege to describe in early America. His classic, *Democracy in America*, is to this day one of the finest explorations of the philosophy of freedom—and yet Tocqueville had no intention at all of proclaiming a philosophy. He simply wanted to report back to his native France how the American experiment was unfolding. In doing so, he told us Americans who we truly were— and are!

Alexis de Tocqueville, a lawyer and an aristocrat, traveled America four decades after Burke died in 1797. Yet the Frenchman saw Burke's vision being lived out wherever he went. He began where Burke began, with religion. The young writer marveled that for the citizens of the young United States, Christian conviction "does not spring from that barren traditionary faith which seems to vegetate in the soul rather than to live."[10] He wrote, "The Americans combine the notions of Christianity and of liberty so intimately in their minds, that it is impossible to make them conceive the one without the other."[11]

Tocqueville saw that it was this firmly held Christianity that kept Americans from sinking into a mean-spirited and soul-killing individualism. He did not find every man out to gain for himself in the young country. Instead, he saw them banding together, building those "voluntary associations" we've talked about, and realizing that if they were going to rise as individuals, they would have to serve the community to help it rise as well. This is one of the often neglected engines of American greatness, and if we're going to continue to be great today we're going to have to protect our communities and private organizations from the destroying hand of the ever-controlling state. Always, we should seek to leave things in better shape than we found them.

Conservatives are inspired by Tocqueville because he located the greatness of America not in mechanisms of government primarily, but in its culture. He talked a great deal about morals and habits. He used the word *mores* often. It means the ways of a community, its character and customs. In other words, he found the reasons for the country's success in what the *people were doing*, not what the government was doing to or for the people. In his native France, government had been everything, the focus of all national life. In the young United States, the *life of the people* created the life of the nation and made it a success.

In fact, he celebrated the limited nature of American government. He said that our federal form of government gave America "the power of a great republic and the security of a small one."[12] He was thrilled to see that local institutions checked what might have been the grasping hand of democracy and instead gave the people "both taste for freedom and the skill to be free."[13] He loved our local government, our free press, our independent judiciary, and the fiery respect he witnessed for individual rights.

What is so powerful about *Democracy in America*, and encouraging, is that it confirmed how a philosophy of freedom had taken up residence in American soil and was working. Four decades into our national life, an insightful visitor from France found all our national distinctives on display. Given what much of Europe had become by this time, we were indeed a *Novus Ordo Seclorum*—a "New Order of the Ages."

We weren't by any means perfect, of course. It was just as Tocqueville was touring America, taking note of our horrid slavery, that England was abolishing slavery with the stroke of a pen. This was largely due to the tireless work of British evangelicals like William Wilberforce. Tragically, the United States would choose instead to fight a bloody civil war that would rend the country even to this day and cost more than seven hundred thousand American lives.

It was in this same decade that Native Americans were removed from their homeland—largely because white men had discovered gold near Echota, the Cherokee lands in Georgia—and forced to march to Oklahoma. During that infamous and vicious "Trail of Tears," as many as half of the sixteen thousand Native Americans died. The United States was no Eden for them.

There were other flaws and failures. Yet it was also true that something new and noble was happening in the world. A new nation was wrung from the hands of one of the most powerful nations on earth and was established on faith in God, individual freedom, rule of law, limited government, free commerce, and all the checks and balances that would keep evil at bay and allow our republic to last. There had simply been nothing like it in the world before. It was a miracle, quite literally, and we ought to be grateful every day despite the fact we must also keep pressing every day toward fulfilling the ideals and the promise of our founding.

I'm thankful for what Burke and Tocqueville mean to us today. Burke brought together the philosophy of freedom drawn from history and sent it into the American experience on soaring rhetoric. Tocqueville confirmed the early success of the American vision, though he was clear-eyed about our challenges and our flaws. I honor them both. They laid a foundational understanding of the conservatism I live out each moment of my life.

Yet I also admire them for another reason. Tocqueville died in 1849. This means that all the great heritage of western conservative thought that Burke expressed so beautifully and Tocqueville so powerfully described came to bear upon the middle of the 1800s. This was a special time for people like me. Important questions were just then being asked in the United States and elsewhere. Why shouldn't women vote? Why shouldn't they hold office? What was it that kept them from own and inheriting property? What was it inherently about a woman that made her less than a man?

These were the questions on millions of minds. Americans were wondering aloud why their statesmen hadn't done as Abigail Adams, wife of founding father John Adams, asked her husband to do when he was serving in the Continental Congress: "Remember the ladies."

Her request at that time is important, so much so that we should read it in its context.

I long to hear that you have declared an independence. And, by the way, in the new code of laws which I suppose it will be necessary for you to make, I desire you would remember the ladies and be more generous and favorable to them than your ancestors. Do not put such unlimited power into the hands of the husbands. Remember, all men would be tyrants if they could. If particular care and attention is not paid to the ladies, we are determined to foment a rebellion, and will not hold ourselves bound by any laws in which we have no voice or representation.[14]

The letter was dated March 31, 1776. These were strong sentiments for that or any day.

By the mid-1880s, the suffragist movement was gaining strength. Women were beginning to claim as their right the liberties the conservative philosophy had so long extolled. It would be only a few decades before women would vote for the first time in the United States.

You probably think I'm referring to the ratification of the Nineteenth Amendment, which gave women the right to vote in 1920. As much as I'm grateful for that moment, that's not the one I'm talking about. Did you know that women in Wyoming were granted suffrage in 1869? On September 6, 1870, Louisa Ann Swain became the first woman to vote. Women in Wisconsin could vote in school-related elections as early as 1884. Prior to this, the thinking in that state and others had been, as the *Milwaukee Journal Sentinel* wrote in a May 31, 1849, "Women are confessedly angels, and angels do not vote."

Well, we are both angels and voters now, and it all started in the mid- to late 1800s when the philosophy of freedom finally began applying to women, too.

You see, women had almost always been conservatives. They knew what was best for their children. They understood what made communities safe. They knew when their town and state were thriving. They realized—often more than their fathers and husbands—what taxes did to a family, how government policies affected the price of things at the store, and how vital faith was to the well-being of a nation. They saw close up almost every day what low morals or irresponsibility or addiction or unwise spending did to a home and to a city. They were cultural conservatives before they were allowed to be political conservatives, and when the opportunity arrived to be both, they took it.

And conservative women soared. The first woman elected

to the U.S. House of Representatives was Jeannette Pickering Rankin. She was a Republican from Montana and, boy, did she make a mark. By the way, she was elected to Congress in 1916, almost four years before the Nineteenth Amendment was made law. This means she was elected by men, which was pretty amazing given that she was an outspoken suffragist, and she introduced the legislation that became the Nineteenth Amendment—nicknamed the Susan B. Anthony Amendment—giving women the vote.

Representative Rankin was elected to the House again in 1940. She became so irritated with the denigrating way that some members of Congress would refer to her as "the lady from Montana" that she took to shouting, "I'm no lady. I'm a member of Congress!" I've always loved her for that.

And so it began. Women began taking their place in the governing of their nation. Many of them had grit, too. In 1925, Florence Kahn, a California Republican, became the fifth female representative in our country. She won a special election for the seat long held by her husband, who had died not long before Florence decided to run. This amazing lady was also Jewish. Think about the kind of opposition she must have faced in her day. Yet she always did it with style. When she was once asked why she was so successful in her work, she replied simply, "Sex appeal!" Oh, imagine saying that. Gotta love it!

Women began taking their places in both the House and the Senate. The women conservatives during this era are some of my heroes. Margaret Chase Smith of Maine was a Republican who served in both the House and the Senate. She was the firebrand who famously stood up against the tactics of Joseph McCarthy. I could describe such women for pages. What is important is that the dam was broken down and women possessed of conservative sensibilities began to make their mark upon the government of our nation.

What a pageant of brains and beauty, wisdom and wonderment it has been. We have been blessed with women like Jeane Kirkpatrick, diplomat and political scientist, a prime architect of Ronald Reagan's foreign policy. Kellyanne Conway is special counsel to President Trump, and Sarah Huckabee Sanders served as the White House press secretary. There is Nikki Haley, governor of South Carolina and former ambassador to the United Nations, and Governor Kristi Noem of South Dakota. There have long been women who are conservative scholars, and they are the grandmothers of today's conservative firebrands like Mollie Hemingway, Ann Coulter, Laura Ingraham, and Candace Owens, the young African American lady who is leading a Black exit—she calls it "Blexit"—out of the Democratic Party.

Speaking of African Americans, I'm grateful for Alveda

King, the niece of Dr. Martin Luther King Jr., who has served in the Georgia House of Representatives and who is an outstanding conservative voice at the Alexis de Tocqueville Institution in Washington, DC. Thank God for the changes that have come in our country. And thank God for conservative Black women like Star Parker, Mia Love, and Kay Cole James. Always, of course, there is the amazing Condoleezza Rice, scholar of Russian history and politics, former secretary of state, and currently the chancellor at Stanford University.

It was thinking of this heritage that moved me so much when I was sworn in as a United States senator. If you've seen the video of my swearing-in ceremony on YouTube, I'm sure you noticed that I cried my way through it. I can't apologize. I have a sense of what it cost pioneer conservative women for me to get where I am. I definitely have a sense of what all women have had to endure through the centuries, simply being women in a society that would not let them be heard. I am grateful for every speech, every article, every book, every vote, and every casual conversation that changed the culture and allowed women to achieve. Somebody finally decided to "remember the ladies," as Abigail Adams charged her husband, and it has made all the difference in the United States and the western world.

Conservatism is not the rich and powerful desperately clinging to their privilege. It is not a movement devoted to erecting barriers against the poor, the foreign, or the disadvantaged. It is a philosophy of freedom. It is what works. It is the counsel of the ages telling us the lessons of what has been tried, what has proven successful, and what has failed and brought human misery. It is the philosophy born of standing on the shoulders of thinking giants and carrying their vision into the future.

This is a bit of the noble heritage of conservatism. Now, it is time for all conservatives, both men and women, to win hearts and minds to this philosophy of freedom in our time.

Chapter Seven

A Caucus of One

How well I remember the initial sting of that phrase: "a caucus of one." I first heard it during my days in the Tennessee state Senate. One of my colleagues was giving a media interview after I had bested him in a skirmish during that now-epic state income tax battle. He was justifying the loss and trying to denigrate my efforts. He sourly told a reporter that I was a "caucus of one," that nobody in the state senate even listened to me.

At first it hurt. No one wants to hear such words, even from their political enemies. Eventually, though, I laughed. Though I had forgotten it for a moment, thousands of Tennesseans were obviously listening to me. Why, most of the state was opposed to an income tax! Moreover, I had just beaten this guy in his attempt to cut a deal and pass a tax despite the expressed will of the people. What's more, he had all the media and the political establishment with him, as well as most of the crowd on Capitol Hill. Despite all this, he was defeated! Of course he had to justify the loss. The caucus of one had taken down his push for a tax.

I might have been a caucus of one, but I was a caucus of one with thousands of Tennesseans behind her! I could handle that.

I have to confess, looking back all these years later, that I was indeed a caucus of one. I was the only female Republican in the state senate at the time. I was also constantly at the tip of the spear in the major policy fights that rocked our state for years, not days, weeks, or months, but years—fights like the ones for lowering government spending and ending driver's licenses for illegal aliens. I was just one person, but I learned something important in those battles: Standing as one is not standing alone. One voice can change a community, state, or even a country. One committed voice can make an historic difference.

Over time, I have come to realize the power in some famous words attributed to Samuel Adams: "It does not take a majority to prevail...but rather an irate tireless minority keen on setting brushfires of freedom in the minds of men."

There is a painting I have in my home that always makes me think of these words. It portrays a solitary figure, a farmer, walking down a country lane. One day my daughter, while looking at the painting, said, "This makes me sad." To her eyes, being alone on a country road was an unhappy and depressing thought. To me, it represents challenge and opportunity. It represents a solitary but valiant soul taking on what life brings.

If you are a caucus of one or the lone champion of a point of view, then you have the opportunity to be the leader, to build a following and grow an idea or a cause from infancy to maturity. You have the chance to turn a country lane into an interstate full of people and ideas. The truth in almost every heroic pursuit is that someone has to be the first. Someone has to be the point of the spear. True, it can mean big risk, but it also brings big reward when you have fought and then won.

During the Tennessee state income tax battle, I had many sleepless nights when I wondered quietly if I had chosen the correct path. We all have our doubts. We all have our dark nights of the soul. Yet in my heart, I knew that what I was doing was best for the state. Certainly, time would prove that a majority of the people in Tennessee agreed. I was also thrilled that some of the fiercest opponents to the tax, fighting right beside me, were women who served in the statehouse: Donna Barrett, Mae Beavers, Diane Black—we formed the Killer Bs and never hesitated to push back on the pro-tax advocates.

Women find themselves in this position regularly. It might

be in their family, church, or work but often their vision is twenty-twenty on an issue. It is clear to them what should be done. Yet they feel they are the only one who gets it. There is something in their souls that tells them they are correct; therefore, they stand firm. We've all heard the phrase "Mother knows best." Well, she often does, and if she was like my mother, she gives others a moral compass and the courage of conviction that will carry them through to victory and to success in valuable causes. This was certainly my mother's gift to me, and it's why the words "caucus of one" don't sting anymore. Now, they are a badge of honor.

———————————

I will tell you, though, that as comfortable as I am with being called a caucus of one, I much prefer to work with people of differing views. I much prefer, as they say in Washington, working bipartisan and bicameral. It means working with the other political party and also with the other chamber of Congress. This is what's best for the country and it is often more enjoyable.

Of the many awards I've been graced with in my life, one of the dearest to me is the one I received from the Ripon Society in 2018. It was their award for bipartisanship and bipartisan accomplishment. Part of the reason I felt especially honored is found in one of the stories that comes from the society's history.

The Ripon Society was founded in 1962 by a group of Massachusetts conservatives. It is named for Ripon, Wisconsin, the birthplace of the Republican Party. They met in that first year in various locations on the Harvard University campus with a goal of promoting wise conservative ideas.

A change came in 1963. Members of the Ripon Society were meeting for lunch at a Harvard dining hall. The business at hand was planning a trip to campaign for Nelson Rockefeller. As the meeting drew to an end, they heard the news that John F. Kennedy had been shot.

Kennedy had been an inspiration to the members of the Ripon Society despite their political differences with him. While grieving the president's death, and fearing the presidency of Lyndon B. Johnson, the society decided to write a manifesto. It was entitled "A Call to Excellence in Leadership: An Open Letter to the New Generation of Republicans." Calling for moderation over extremism, bipartisan cooperation over politics as total war, the manifesto put the Ripon Society onto the national stage and even won public praise from former president Dwight Eisenhower.

The society continues to represent "reaching across the aisle" to this day, and I am deeply honored to have received their award and to be on their advisory board. It reminds me that some of my most satisfying moments in politics have been when I was allowed to work with people I did not agree with to get something important done.

I've long said that our nation and our freedom is bolstered by robust respectful bipartisan debate. It is essential. It is also true that laws that are made through bipartisan participation are laws that last. As you look at our nation's history, you find that partisan line votes yield laws and policies that end up being reworked or even repealed. They don't have the buy-in and support that allows them to last through the years and do the good they were intended to do. My thought is that anything worth doing is worth doing right the first time. It saves time, energy, and the taxpayers' money. For that reason, I like working with those I don't necessarily agree with on every issue.

Indeed my first big political battle saw me standing in opposition to our Tennessee governor, a man I held and still hold in high regard and whom I had even campaigned to elect. I was also in opposition to the political establishment, many of the legislators, lobbyists, and groups that sought favor with the state government. While increased taxes are usually an idea of the left, I found a receptive audience to my opposition to higher taxes among some Tennesseans who identified as Democrats but who also opposed a tax hike. It was a matter of principle to them. They did not want a new tier of taxes piled on top of the taxation and regulation they already faced in their businesses. They understood well the famous maxim that the power to tax is the power to destroy. They had seen taxes destroy Tennessee's businesses time and again.

During that four-year fight, many of the lessons learned were mine, beginning with the importance of keeping an open mind and always reaching out. It was during this time that I learned the value of investing time to have a conversation with anyone who wanted to make the lives of Tennesseans better. I put every organizational and communications skill I had developed into leading this effort and defeating this tax. I did not have a big staff or big budget. It was important to educate and involve the citizens of our state to win this fight. It is because of thousands of Tennesseans of every political stripe that we have no state income tax today, and as a result the state is thriving. It was people of both parties who made it happen. Many of the folks from the other side of the aisle who fought at my side in that tax fight are still dear friends today.

In 2016, a bipartisan coalition was successful in crafting and seeing President Barack Obama sign into law an important piece of health care research legislation entitled 21st Century Cures. It was developed to chart a pathway for personalized medicine and to incentivize research on rare and debilitating diseases such as Alzheimer's, rare cancers, and ALS. I can't tell you how rewarding this was, even more because I had worked with friends across the aisle to bring it about.

This inspired me toward even more bipartisan, bicameral efforts. I authored a piece of legislation called the Software Act with a Democratic colleague. This legislation established the statutory definition for health technology, pathways for approval of health apps, and methods for reimbursement for health technology services. Another Democratic colleague and I wrote the Kids Count Act, which allows children to be included in clinical trials. Each of these bipartisan efforts, which were included in the 21st Century Cures law, produced immense good and leaves me convinced that this is the type of collaboration that we need to have more of in Washington today.

When I became a U.S. senator, it occurred to me that we were approaching the centennial celebration of women's suffrage. I decided we needed to have a specially minted silver dollar coin to commemorate the occasion. By working across the aisle, I saw every woman in the Senate join me in helping to pass the bill, and then I had the privilege of seeing it passed by the House. Again, bipartisan and bicameral. It is true, such bipartisan efforts do take more work, but it is worth the price given the way worthy causes are given long lives when championed by leaders in both parties and in both chambers of Congress.

I've seen equally encouraging results in my work on privacy. Since we live in a technological world, I have worked tirelessly on the issue of online privacy to be certain that you have the tools in your toolbox to protect the "virtual you"— you and your presence online. No one wants a snoop sorting through their browser history or picking key words from their emails or following their children on an app. No one wants to be spammed, but this is the kind of thing that big tech is allowing to happen. They do it to you every day. Therefore, I worked with a diverse coalition to push forward the Browser Act, and develop a light-touch data-privacy and data-security standard to keep you and your family safe online.

———————————

Now, I would like to tell you that all of my work in politics has been on a bipartisan, bicameral basis. It's hasn't been. In fact, it can't be. I wish it could. The simple fact is that politics in America is becoming more heated and contentious than ever. While our founding fathers built a certain degree of tension and conflict into our governmental system, I think they would be shocked by what is happening today.

First, let's celebrate the good. We would not be having

policy discussions—heated or not—if it weren't for the Constitution, which allows us to freely express our opinions and have an open debate in the public square without fear of retribution from our government. The ability to petition our government, to express our opinions and access our elected officials, is among the rights most treasured by the American people. I regularly hear from Tennesseans who want to weigh in on a policy issue. They want to make their point of view known, and I listen whether I agree or not. I believe that our nation and our representative republic have been well served by robust respectful political debate. It is what enables us to arrive at consensus and find a way to protect our freedoms.

It is also why we have two major parties—one that tilts toward individual freedom, and another that tilts toward a larger government role. We have one that is for a smaller, decentralized government and another that is for a bigger, more centralized form of government. We have one that wants a lower tax burden and another that calls for a larger tax burden to fund big government. There is one that believes in a larger military, and another that demands a much smaller military. The list goes on. Yet what separates us from so many other countries is that we discuss, debate, and argue until we hit the right blend of ideas. Then we make the laws.

All of this has worked well since the founding of our

country. It has worked well, that is, until we began to see the media not just report the news, but report with bias and turn journalism into advocacy. This relatively recent trend was exacerbated and accelerated by the gift of the internet. The words "I read it on the internet so it must be true" became a constant refrain. I can't tell you how much misinformation and disinformation has been spread in the virtual space by people either ignorant or ill intentioned. We see it every day in policy issues that range from border security to childhood vaccines. Today we are not only dealing with differing opinions, we are dealing with absolute falsehoods that people believe are true and would stake their lives on. The sad fact is that they just might be *actually* staking their lives on these lies given the vital, life-and-death issues we are dealing with these days and the stunning misinformation out there about them.

It is an important time for cooler heads to prevail. It is an important time for the values of the Ripon Society to step to the fore. Obviously, not all Democrats are leftists any more than all Republicans are right-wingers. There are scores of people who are in the middle and who are moderates. There is also the slightly right-of-center crowd. What has happened with the growth of opinion journalism, Hollywood activism, and the dark and misinformed side of the internet is that the ideology of the left has been given a massive echo chamber that pushes their positions. It creates the narrative of "this is what's best for the country and if you are really cool, this is what is best for you. You should choose to express this opinion and this opinion only." I can tell you that dealing with such attitudes is exhausting—but I suppose that this is exactly the point!

It is no wonder surveys report that millennials believe the earth is going up in flames due to global warming. It is no wonder so many Americans think that conservatives with money are evil because they support lower taxes and want all Americans to have the right to keep their hard-earned dollars. And in the reality-distortion field of the left, it makes perfect sense that stabilizing Medicare and Social Security for future generations is nothing more than a scheme for taking money away from the elderly. This makes about as much sense as the idea that being against abortion is about taking away a woman's right to choose and is not really about saving lives.

I would love to work more with people on the other side of the aisle as I often have in the past, but I have to tell you that the methods of the left make me and other conservatives suspicious. There is a deceptive element. There is a sneakiness. I suppose the more sophisticated word for it is *incrementalism.*

The American political left does not strive to win its policy wars openly. It doesn't want that level of scrutiny, that level of light shining in hidden corners. Instead, the left chooses its battles very carefully and with the intent of moving the line of big-government control just a little bit at a time. They are smart and they choose their language and their issues well. They have made leftist progress in this country by executing precisely this strategy—inch by inch, policy by policy, ever growing government while saying they are doing something completely different.

The examples of their progress are everywhere. From activist judges on the court to left-leaning policies in education, environment, and health care, the political left makes its biggest gains when they make repeated—and often covert— small gains. The tragedy is that they make these gains in the name of trying to find compromise or so called bipartisanship. But to them, there is no compromise. They just keep moving ever leftward—ever toward greater government control, ever toward loss of individual rights, ever toward higher taxes and a restriction of the private sector.

I've seen the pattern repeated numerous times. They stake out a far-left position, further than anyone would imagine possible. Then, they aggressively argue their point and claim that the political right is misrepresenting the outcomes that could result from their policies. When they finally do arrive at what they almost laughingly refer to as "consensus," they will have agreed to it only because the new policy moves the federal government even further to the left than it was before. And *left* is a code word for more power to the government and a loss of freedom for you. Then they declare victory and praise those on the right who worked with them to find agreement. Behind the scenes, though, they call the folks on the right who tried in good faith to work with them "dupes" or "useful idiots," in Vladimir Lenin's famous and chilling phrase.

This process constantly repeats itself not only at the federal but also at the state and local level. It frustrates conservatives and libertarians who want less government. They realize that leftist victories do nothing but give big government the power to make decisions for the people and provide all the people's basic needs, all while taking away rights and dramatically expanding the size of government. It happens nearly every time.

I'll tell you what the real problem is with this, besides ever-growing government control. It is that bipartisanship and a bicameral approach are lost. To be honest, those of us on the other side of the aisle from the liberals simply cease to trust them anymore. We would like to work together for the good of the nation, but we pretty much know that any head fake from liberals toward working in a bipartisan way is little more than cover for their agenda of ever-creeping government control over all of life.

The policies of liberals grow like an infestation. They are quiet and below the surface, then you pull back the cover and there they are. Working out of sight. Changing how you work and live, and you never knew it was happening.

The slippery slope of progressivism has been picking up steam for decades. When you look at post–World War I American politics, you can easily track their work. The New Deal, the Great Society, and now the Green New Deal are all about tilting the nation leftward.

Honestly, I sometimes wish Republicans would be as aggressive in fighting back against the left as the Democrats are in fighting back against the right. With the liberals' passion for giving control and power to a few and for centralizing authority, they think they have won if they can get just one more inch on a given front—from gun rights to labor policy, minimum wage to women's rights and the workplace, pay equity or privacy.

All these things sound harmless, perhaps, until they pave the way for more and more government control. Every time government steps in to do a job or fill a need—which is the same thing as saying every time the government grows—you, the citizen, have to give up some of your rights and freedoms.

And liberals never announce their true intentions. They just creep along doing damage—incrementally—and hope you won't notice.

While I love working across the aisle with people who are sincere and achieving great things for our country, I'm willing to be a caucus of one if I have to be. Part of the reason I'm willing is that there are some issues that are so important to me and that I believe are so critical to the life of our nation that I'll champion them even if I'm the only one on earth who does. Let me tell you about a few of these.

The first—and perhaps the most desperate—is the issue of life and abortion. I want you to allow a single fact to sink into your mind and soul. Every day in America, around 1,700 babies are killed. They are pulled from the womb and murdered. Some are cut into pieces, some are crushed. And, as we learned from the diabolical videos of Planned Parenthood executives making deals over a glass of wine a few years ago, some of them are split open so that their little organs can be harvested and sold to the highest bidder who logs into the seller's website and orders up the fetal tissue—brain, arms, heart—at a certain gestational age. As chair of the Select Panel on Infant Lives, I was horrified as I read these reports and reviewed this info.

This goes on every day in America. Now, think about what would happen in this country if members of some group other than the unborn were being murdered at an average of 1,700 a day.[1] Picture any combination of age, gender, station, or ethnicity. There would be an almost violent uproar. It would, rightly, be declared a national emergency and would be the main topic of nearly every news report, political debate, or campaign for office in the land. It would be a horrifying holocaust and deserve every bit of our national attention.

Yet, according to the Centers for Disease Control, 1,700 children are taken from the womb every day for the single purpose of ending their lives and somehow those like me who dare to bring it up are thought to be evil. It is said that we want to limit women's rights. We are anti-feminist. We want the government to intrude into women's bodies. We are reactionary and fetus worshippers and right-wing extremists.

Seventeen hundred babies. Every day. In America. And all legal.

I have often been moved by these words from our Declaration of Independence: "We hold these Truths to be self-evident, that all Men are created equal, that they are endowed by their Creator with certain unalienable Rights, that among these are Life, Liberty, and the Pursuit of Happiness." It is a magnificent sentiment expressed with breathtaking beauty. And what

comfort and assurance it is to know that our founding generation listed the Right to Life first in its list of inalienable rights
that belong to all men.

I loved these words from the Declaration from the moment
I first heard them, but I came to hold them even dearer through
an unexpected experience I had when I was in high school. In
those days, I played the piano for my church. I delighted in
doing that job—playing for services and choir rehearsals, preparing music for the offertory, and, of course, all the preparation for special holidays. It took most of my free time but I was
never as happy as when I was at the keyboard. Those moments
truly consumed me with joy. I thrilled to use my gifts for God.
I also loved the opportunities my work in music gave me to
exercise my faith.

One of the most life-changing of these came when my
church issued a call for help with a Sunday afternoon worship
service for residents at the Ellisville State School, a facility for
those with mental illness located about twenty minutes from
my home. As soon as I heard the announcement, I knew I was
supposed to volunteer. So, on Sunday afternoons I played the
piano for that sweet worship service while my friend Jimmy
Knight led the singing. As the final notes of our last song faded
away, Ray Moffett then stepped up and delivered the lessons.
I'm grateful for all the good that I saw come of that time of

ministry and love. Yet, surprisingly, one of the most important results of those Sunday afternoons for me had to do with my understanding of the sanctity of life.

The reason is that many of those who attended the service at Ellisville had Down syndrome. As I got to know them, I was always struck by how happy they were, how productive they seemed to be and in their own special way. Their sweet spirit and joyous singing would thrill me. A couple of the girls who were regular attendees would often sit on the piano bench next to me, one hand on my back and the other resting on top of mine as we played the hymns together. We played the piano, we sang with joy, and every Sunday I choked back joyous tears of understanding.

Their delight spoke volumes. I could feel their deep love, could sense their understanding and emotional depth. I remember thinking often of how precious their lives must be to God and what a delight they must also be to their parents and their other family members. Against all this I had to hold up the dark truth that Down syndrome babies are often aborted. When this genetic disorder is detected in a child in the womb, some doctors routinely urge mothers to abort to prevent the burden to the family and the struggle of a life that is not—well, normal.

Yet I could never escape the thought, "Who are we to play

God? Who are we to say that such lives are not beautiful and productive and meaningful in their own way? Where did we get the right to decide who deserves death and before even one day of these lives is lived?" So, during my teenage Sunday afternoons, when most of my friends were out somewhere playing, I learned the lesson that every life is precious and intentional in God's plan. Each life has a purpose.

So you can imagine why I am opposed to the pro-abortion agenda of Planned Parenthood. I'm all for its other medical services to women, yet Planned Parenthood is the largest provider of abortion services in the United States. Given what I see in our Declaration of Independence, given what I know of God's love and what those very special friends taught me all those years ago, I cannot be anything but disgusted by the lives destroyed by Planned Parenthood's tragic agenda.

It is the arrogance of this organization that gets me most. They dare to tell mothers that they have the right to decide if the child they bear should live or die. It sounds barbaric when stated like this, but the basic premise of the pro-abortion position is just that. No matter the varying opinions of when life begins, when a child is aborted, a life is ended. Always. Forever.

It's very interesting to me—given the insults and abuse that those of us who are pro-life have to endure—that this is a policy issue in which science is on our side. I've had conversations with numerous women who were fashionably pro-choice until they saw the sonogram of their grandchild. Some of these grandmothers remembered God's words in Psalm 139, that he knew us in the womb before one day of our lives was lived. As they stared at those sonogram images and looked tearfully into the faces of their unborn grandchildren, these women understood as though for the first time that the child before them had a divine purpose. That heartbeat, that face, was ordained. God had chosen. God had prepared. God had given life. None of these women could remain pro-abortion after that experience. Now, we were talking about their grandchild! A life!

In 2015 and 2016, when I was still in the House, I chaired the Select Investigative Panel. We were charged with gathering facts on the selling of fetal tissues and baby body parts. Some abortion clinics and tissue merchants had formed business partnerships around aborted fetuses. Given the evil we were commissioned to address, we worked exceptionally hard. It was difficult work given how hard traffickers in fetal organs work to conceal their crimes, and frankly, it was sickening to see what can happen to the young. Yet we gathered the important information we needed and then we turned fifteen criminal referrals over to the Department of Justice. That was one of the hardest yet most rewarding assignments I ever had in the House of Representatives.

What was shocking during this time was the vicious nature of the pro-abortion left. Threats to my staff, my family, and to me became weekly occurrences. I suspect the reason was that Planned Parenthood had grown to be a billion-dollar business and we were onto their game. They clearly had an agenda in keeping abortion rates high in America: They were offering the bodies of aborted fetuses in exchange for the dollars they brought into their coffers. Truly disgusting.

By the way, I should mention that Planned Parenthood receives around a half billion dollars of your tax money every year. I think it's time for this to stop!

So, you can see why I'm so fierce in my defense of the rights of the unborn. Be a caucus of one in their behalf if I must? Yes. No question!

Another national issue I'm passionate about is immigration. Many Americans have been programmed by liberals into thinking that those of us who want wise immigration are cold-hearted about human suffering and want to undo our Ellis Island–type legacy in this country. Nothing could be further from the truth. Let's preserve it!

Every time I talk about the issue of illegal immigration, I think of the angel moms and families whom I've met, the grief they live with on a daily basis, and how truly unfair the process has become. Wendy Corcoran from Knoxville, Tennessee, is one of those angel moms. Her son, Pierce, was driving just days before New Year's Eve in 2018 and was hit by a forty-four-year-old illegal alien named Francisco Eduardo Franco-Cambrany. Pierce was killed on impact.

Oddly, no field sobriety or breathalyzer test was conducted at the scene. In time, then, the case against Franco-Cambrany slowed and ultimately he was deported back to Mexico. He was never tried, and there are no reports of any legal ramifications. Wendy Corcoran lost her beloved son and no justice was done. It is all because the man who crashed into her son that horrible night was an illegal alien. I'm sure I don't have to tell you how completely unfair, even un-American, all this is.

It is true that America is a melting pot. Yet it is not here merely to pass out tickets for free entry. Our sovereignty and our citizenship are priceless. If we don't take care of it, we all suffer, and that is what happens when illegal immigration is allowed to continue. It puts those intent upon disobeying our laws in the queue ahead of those who are legally entering.

Is it fair for someone to evade the system, come in illegally, and reap the benefits of citizenship while living outside the law? Should they be allowed to get a driver's license, send their children to school, work, own property, and have health care just because they found a way to get around our laws and get inside our borders? Should we encourage cities and states to defy the federal government and become sanctuaries for illegal aliens who want to evade the law and provide cover for drug, sex, and human trafficking cartels and gangs that inflict harm on innocent citizens?

Of course not. It is not fair to the citizens of the United States. Nor is it faithful to our American system of government.

Just because you want to do something does not mean you can or should do it—and this applies to illegal immigration. If someone wants to come to our country to live and work, they should do so by following our laws and rules and become contributing members of society. I have many friends who are legal immigrants and naturalized citizens. They have spent both time and money to achieve legal status, and they are proud of that accomplishment. They are some of the staunchest advocates for securing our border, tightening our standards, increasing vetting, and being sure we know who comes into our country and why. As naturalized citizens, they know the value of American citizenship.

Yet many who come to our shores simply want to game the system, to benefit from our bountiful country while contributing nothing. One of the most egregious forms of gaming the immigration system is the issue of "anchor babies" and "birthright tourism." Both of these occur when people who aren't Americans make sure their babies are born in the United States so that their children receive the full benefits of American citizenship. Our laws regarding this are so ineffectual that there is an actual industry serving wealthy women who want to have their babies in the United States. A firm secures visas for these women; they travel here in style, stay in the finest hotels, and then have their babies in our hospitals. And, POOF! Those babies are citizens of the United States—simply by virtue of where their mothers were at their birth. There is no love of country. There is no valuing of what it means to be an American. There is no contribution to our society. Yet now their baby is able to benefit from all it means to be an American when all that has happened is that the mother has dropped by for a few days. It is a travesty.

The system has to change. We must raise the standards for what it means to become an American. In my opinion, it is imperative that we secure our borders and our ports of entry. It is a must that we end chain migration, that we lower the caps for refugees, and that we increase vetting standards. These are all issues that I am working on. It is also important that we reform the legal immigration system. Use of biometrics— of biological information like DNA, for example—allows the Border Patrol to know if a person is who they claim to be and thus lets us know who is coming into the country. Also essential is the tracking of individuals who are here on visas and then insisting that they exit when the visa expires. Did you know that most of the 9/11 hijackers originally came with a passport and a visa but did not exit once their visa expired? We don't need a repeat of that tragedy.

Don't misunderstand me here. We certainly need seasonal farm workers. Our businesses need high-tech workers. Factories need employees to supplement their workforces. We want the good things immigration brings to our land. This is a far different thing, though, from people illegally entering our country, committing crimes, benefitting from our largesse, and contributing nothing. The day of that being allowed must come to an end.

So why does such abuse of the right of citizenship exist in our country? It is because the American political left has sold acceptance of illegal immigration as a compassion issue, saying we should open our arms and welcome those who are trying to establish better lives for themselves. We should greet them with warm hearts and help them settle in. Well, compassion is a two-way street. If you want to say that illegal immigrants should be welcomed compassionately and treated like everyone else, then what do you say to the mom who has lost a child, the spouse who is now alone, the law enforcement officer who puts on her uniform every night and prays that illegal alien gangs don't create havoc in her community? What do you say to the parent whose child is addicted to the drugs that flood our streets because they are being delivered by illegal cartels through illegal immigrants?

Likewise, what do you tell the Central American parent who has not seen their child since they paid the cartel to bring them in the United States? Think of it. Mom and Dad haven't heard a word. They are anxious, but they probably don't realize that their child is possibly now in a gang or a human trafficking ring. What do you tell the ten-year-old girl who was raped during her journey to our border?

How is any of this fair or righteous or American? Let's open our arms and hearts to those who come here legally and want to abide by our laws. Let's stand beside those who have been persecuted for their religious beliefs. But let's not allow illegal entry to continue as a common and accepted practice.

You see, then, that as with the issue of abortion, I'm willing to be a caucus of one if I have to be in order to see illegal immigration ended. My critics will say I'm racist. They will say I'm a privileged woman who does not want others to have her opportunities. Of course, none of it is true. Yet I'm willing to take the heat for what I believe. I do not take the stands I take for my own good and privilege. I take them because I love this country, because I have taken a sacred oath to protect it, and because I believe in a God who calls me to truth, who calls me to ethical compassion, and who calls me to stand against the immoral folly of my age.

Let me give you an example of one moral stand I take. Have you looked at the national debt lately? It is over $22 trillion and climbing every second, minute, hour of every day. Every child born as a citizen of this country has their share of the national debt: "Welcome to the world. You are now responsible for $60,000 in US debt."

Is it fair to future generations to overspend today and cause them to bear the burden of a national debt that is going to rocket their federal income tax rate, business taxes, and governmental fees into the stratosphere? I believe it is immoral to push this debt to our children and grandchildren. We should deal with it now by passing a balanced budget amendment to the Constitution that requires us to balance the books without a tax increase on hardworking Americans. We should require the federal bureaucracy to shrink and agencies to be more accountable to the people they are supposed to be serving.

This is one of the primary differences between liberals, libertarians, and conservatives.

Liberals want government to be the first to provide our needs.

Conservatives want the rule of law and light-touch regulation.

Libertarians want to live their life free of government interference.

We should all agree with Admiral Michael Mullen's statement in 2010: "The most significant threat to our national security is our debt."[2] It is imperative that we ensure our children the inheritance of a free and prosperous America.

How can I not speak out about such an important issue to our future?

It's easy to write these words. It's harder to live them. It's particularly hard in our day of strident liberalism, the media as echo chamber of the left, and social media that can make fiction sound like fact just through mere repetition. Let me give you a warning, since I'm eager to prepare you for all you will face as a conservative woman. You will be criticized. You will be vilified. You will have to hear the things you like most about yourself twisted and offered as evidence of your flaws to a watching world. Don't let it deter you. Don't let it intimidate you. Who you are and what it will mean to those around you if you live out your values will be worth anything you have to endure.

You may be wondering how I can be certain of this. Well, I've lived through some bruising seasons of my own. Let me tell you now about one of the biggest.

Chapter Eight

Laws and Sausages

The wisest thing ever said about how laws are made was left to us by the great nineteenth century German statesman, Otto von Bismarck. He reportedly remarked, "Laws, like sausages, cease to inspire respect in proportion as we know how they are made."[1] This is the translation from old German. The simpler English way to say it is, "Laws are like sausages. You should never see them being made."

Most Americans know that their laws are made through a complex process and it's a process that is hard to watch. Usually, there is a good and noble purpose at work when a law is first proposed. Then comes the debate, the compromise, and the thousand different agendas that want to hitch a ride on the law's wagon. Some of this is a genuine attempt to help, but much of it isn't. Greed sometimes plays a role, as does ego and regional pride and plain old vain ambition. Before long, the original law doesn't look anything like it did when it was first proposed. It's like a dinner with too many cooks, a painting with too many artists.

Americans tend to have only a vague sense of this. Though our lives are increasingly dominated by politics, as a nation we understand less and less about how politics really works. I'm sorry to say that a great deal of this is the fault of our schools. We don't teach hardcore history, civics, or government much anymore. The curriculum in our schools tends more toward social studies and courses in trendy current causes rather than the truth about what has happened in our country and how our government actually works. A high school graduate, then, might know more about the battle for immigrant rights in the last decade or two than the battle to free the slaves, more about what PETA says about animal rights than about how a bill makes its way through Congress.

Those of us who work in politics fall victim to this knowledge gap time and again. Modern media actually plays to it. They know that it is possible, for example, for a congressman or senator to have to oppose an otherwise good bill because so much pork and silliness have been loaded on it that it would be a travesty to vote for it. Let's say a bill is proposed to help children read better. Senator A likes it. Then the law has to work its way through the pork barrel buffet in Washington, DC. In time, the bill includes requirements that the books for the program have to come from a certain state or that 20 percent of the books read have to be by transgender authors or that parents can't have any say in the materials used for teaching reading to their children. Well, now Senator A has to oppose an otherwise good bill. And the headline in your local newspaper is "Senator A Opposes Child Literacy." This kind of thing happens all the time.

I want to tell you about a time this happened to me. I'm not doing this because my feelings are hurt and I want to strike back. No, I want to do it because it is the kind of thing that most conservative women will have to deal with if they are going to be public about what they believe. I'm hoping you can learn from it. I want you to be better equipped because you draw from the lessons of my experience for experiences of your own.

After serving for sixteen years in the U.S. House of Representatives, in 2018 I decided to run for the U.S. Senate. My friend Bob Corker had decided not to run for another term, and I believed that I had the experience and the determination to serve Tennesseans well in that role. Most folks in my state knew me, knew what I stood for, and knew that I would work tirelessly for their good. I won the Republican primary handily, receiving 84 percent of the vote.

I then faced former two-time governor Phil Bredesen in the general election. He is an easygoing, affable man with whom I had enjoyed a good relationship through the years. Still, I thought Phil was too much under the sway of Democratic Party leaders in Washington, and I thought he was out of step with most Tennesseans. It was a tight battle. Throughout most of the campaign, Phil and I had raised about the same amount of money and had about the same levels of support.

As election day was nearing an unexpected bomb was dropped onto the campaign. Taylor Swift, the amazingly successful young celebrity with hundreds of millions of followers worldwide, announced that she was going to vote for Phil Bredesen. This was unexpected by nearly everyone, including Bredesen, because Taylor had strained to keep herself publicly nonpolitical. She had never spoken out on political matters before and she had never disclosed anything about her votes. Now, here she was, taking sides late in a heated political battle.

Yet Taylor didn't just announce her support for Phil. She

also announced her disgust for me. She told her 126 million followers on Instagram that my voting record in Congress "appalls and terrifies" her. Then, she let me have it.

> She [Blackburn] voted against equal pay for women. She voted against the Reauthorization of the Violence Against Women Act, which attempts to protect women from domestic violence, stalking, and date rape. She believes businesses have a right to refuse service to gay couples. She also believes they should not have the right to marry. These are not MY Tennessee values. I will be voting for Phil Bredesen for Senate.[2]

Given Taylor's fame, news of this endorsement shot around the country. Nearly every major outlet carried it. And, as you can imagine, Democrats and my opponents at every level made the most of it. Thankfully, I had allies on the right and the left. When asked how he felt about Taylor's endorsement, President Trump joked, "I like her music twenty-five percent less." Former Arkansas governor Mike Huckabee tweeted, "So @taylorswift13 has every right to be political but it won't impact election unless we allow 13 yr old girls to vote. Still with #MarshaBlackburn."[3]

To get the full picture of what was happening around

Taylor at the time, we have to jump ahead a bit. On January 31, 2020, a documentary about the pop star entitled *Miss Americana* was released both on Netflix and in select theaters. Viewers were treated to video from the time that Taylor was choosing to endorse Bredesen, and to video of her offering up more vitriol about me.

During a tearful moment with both her team and her parents, Taylor declares that she is going to take a stand politically. "It's not that I want to step into this," she says. "I just—I can't not at this point." Then, she goes on to explain:

> [Blackburn] votes against the reauthorization of the Violence Against Women Act, which is just basically protecting us from domestic abuse and stalking. Stalking! [Taylor says this as she gestures at herself.] She thinks that if you're a gay couple, or even if you look like a gay couple, you should be allowed to be kicked out of a restaurant. It's really basic human rights, and it's right and wrong at this point, and I can't see another commercial and see her disguising these policies behind the words "Tennessee Christian Values." Those aren't Tennessee Christian values. I live in Tennessee. I am Christian. That's not what we stand for.

And there was more. Before this part of the documentary is over, Taylor calls me "Trump in a Wig," a "racist," a "fascist," and a "homophobe." She also declares that I am "the kind of female males want us to be in a horrendous 1950s world."[4]

Well, let's just say it wasn't the most edifying episode in my political life. Then, of course, I don't look to celebrities for edification!

I should tell you that when the *Miss Americana* documentary was released, I issued a public statement. It read, in part, "Taylor is an exceptionally gifted artist and songwriter, and Nashville is fortunate to be the center of her creative universe." I closed with, "I wish Taylor the best—she's earned it."[5]

I also said that there are some things Taylor and I would agree on. I would look forward to talking to her about them. In fact, let me state right here that I'd be delighted to have Taylor up to my house in Nashville—she'll probably know where it is since it's the former home of the late Sarah Cannon, better known as Minnie Pearl—and talk all this through.

Yet none of this is to shrink from our differences. I'm a Christian. I'm a conservative. I have no intention of backing away from principles I've staked my life on. I believe in marriage and the family unit. I am not at all a homophobe, but I am cautious about the LGBTQ+ political agenda in this country. In fact, I'll leave my defense on this matter to a Washington journalist: "Blackburn's record in Congress may not be one that neatly coincides with Swift's left-wing politics, but it's not at all unusual for a conservative politician. So, no, Blackburn does not appear to be a 'homophobic racist,' and if she's 'Trump in a wig,' that's just because she's not one of the liberals in Swift's ideological bubble."[6]

Before I dive into the more serious matter of the Violence Against Women Act, what else can I dispense with? I was in second grade when the 1950s ended, so I'm not trying to drag us back to that time. I barely remember it! Neither Donald Trump nor I wear a wig. No couple, gay or not, are in danger of being kicked out of a restaurant because of anything I've ever done. I have plenty of friends who are gay, and we don't get kicked out when we grab coffee or lunch. And very few people in American politics, male or female, have worked as hard as I have on behalf of equal pay for women, protection of women from violence, or from stalking. This is why I was honored, during the years I was in the Tennessee state senate, to receive the Voice of the Victims award.

Now for the big reveal about the Violence Against Women Act. Here it is. I voted for it. Yes, I did. In 2013, I voted for that essential bill. Before, that is, it made its way through the Washington pork barrel buffet and ended up looking like a legislative Frankenstein. Trey Gowdy, a former federal prosecutor and former congressman, had this to say on February 28, 2013, about the VAWA legislation after it went through that buffet: "For some women, especially today, the monster is this broken political system that we have, a broken political system which manufactures reasons to oppose otherwise good bills just to deny one side a victory. The House version protects every single American, period. But it will not get a single Democrat vote because it is our version. Welcome to our broken political system."

The Violence Against Women Act was first placed into law in 1994. It was a good act. It had bipartisan support. It provided almost $2 billion to fund prosecution of crimes against women, to require restitution from those convicted of crimes against women, and to ensure that violence against women that prosecutors overlooked could still be tried in civil court. It also established the Office on Violence Against Women in the Department of Justice.

Who could be against that? I wasn't in Congress then, nor was I when the Act was renewed in 2000, as it had to be every few years. Yet this original bill was good solid bipartisan American legislation, all in service of a serious crisis in our country—violent crimes against women.

It is important at this moment that I remind you of what I said at the start of this chapter: Good legislation sometimes goes through such tortured processes that it ends up becoming something even the legislation's original author can't support. Well, that was what started to happen to the Violence Against Women Act. Each time the Act was renewed—in 2000, 2005, and 2013—it was reworked and larded up with other agendas so that it ceased to resemble anything it was originally designed to do.

Let me be clear. I want violence against women stopped. I want the perpetrators punished. I want law enforcement to have all the tools to hunt down the lowlifes who abuse women and end their abuse. I want prosecutors to have the same. I also want abused women to be able to seek redress in civil court, to defend themselves, and to generally have what they need to get healthy and get on with their lives. And, yes, Taylor, I want all provisions necessary to end stalking. Like you, I've been stalked. I carry a gun as a result. I'm glad you have the security a celebrity needs so that you don't have to, but I want all women to have this option if they choose it. This is why I continue to push legislation that will keep women and children safe in both the physical and virtual space.

Now let's take a look at what the Violence Against Women Act had become by the time it came up for reauthorization.

Let's start with the law's definition of what domestic violence is. The law that was in effect before the 2018 reauthorization, U.S. Code 42-13925, used this definition: "The term 'domestic violence' includes felony or misdemeanor crimes of violence committed by a current or former spouse of the victim."[7] Now that language is clear and objective. You can protect women with language like that.

Yet the definition proposed in the 2018 version, HR 6545, was definitely not clear and objective. Here it is: "The term 'domestic violence' means a pattern of behavior involving the use or attempted use of physical, sexual, verbal, emotional, economic, or technological abuse or any other coercive behavior committed, enabled, or solicited to gain or maintain power and control over a victim."[8]

Under this language, domestic violence is no longer limited to crimes of violence. Instead, it can be emotional. It can be most anything one person does to control another person. The language is also subjective. Law enforcement and prosecutors have to figure out the motivation of the suspect rather than use a simple, objective standard: Did he hit her or didn't he?

Think about the unbelievably broad language in the new law. "Verbal, emotional, economic, or technological abuse." These terms are all so vague that it would be almost impossible to determine whether a crime has been committed or not. The language also criminalizes acts that happen in normal, healthy relationships. Is it emotional abuse if one spouse handles the money and doles it out to the other? Is this a tactic to "gain or maintain power and control"—a crime under the new law— or is it simply budgeting? What if a couple have a fight and there is some yelling and door slamming? Is this verbal abuse? You're not sure? Well, you'd better get sure because that argument you had last night with the spouse you love might have been a crime—assuming the language of the 2018 proposal.

It gets worse. What in the world is technological abuse? I don't know and my job is to make laws. I'd certainly understand if law enforcement officials are confused. If a woman reads her husband's emails, is that technological abuse? If I pick up my husband's cell phone and read his texts without his permission, have I committed a crime?

Now, the bill does try to help us with a definition of technological abuse, but it only makes matters worse. Part of this definition tells us that "unwanted, repeated telephone calls, text messages, instant messages, or social media posts" are abusive and therefore a crime. What? Let's say your husband texts you this message: "Babe, where are you? I've been waiting for you for 20 minutes. You're late!" Now, suppose he does it three times. Has he committed a crime under the new language? He's also in danger of prosecution if you have an argument, then he leaves for work and calls you five times while at work, and you have not had a chance to cool off. Unwanted and repeated. Could he be going to jail?

There's more, but let me remind us of how far we've come. This is a law designed to prevent violence toward *women*. Such violence is a plague on our society. We want to stop it—NOW. Yet look at what we're doing. We're swimming around in language like "emotional abuse" and "repeated phone calls." We are far away from the specific issue of violence against women, aren't we? And the more you dilute the definitions and broaden the murky reach of the law, the fewer women who are actual victims will be served. And I can tell you that, as fine as our law enforcement folks are in this country, if they can't figure out what a crime is, they won't arrest and intervene. Understandably. That means that women are badly served by the language of this law. Dangerously!

Clearly, the law was being made weaker. For example, the definition of a "crime of violence" used in the law from the beginning meant the actual, attempted, or threatened use of "physical force." Now that's language that will stop a woman from being beaten and help severely punish the perpetrator. Yet now, as we've seen, this clear definition has been dissolved into "coercive behavior committed, enabled, or solicited to gain or maintain power and control over a victim." Coercive behavior? Maintain power? No one knows what these mean in this context.

The law also can be applied so as to violate the Constitution's guarantee of the "right to keep and bear Arms." Surely we all agree that if anyone ought to have the freedom to exercise this right, it is a woman who is being physically abused. Yet the language of the new law actually makes it possible for a woman, or a man, to have their right to bear arms taken away. This can happen if they are merely notified and have opportunity to appear in court, not if they have actually appeared in court. As the Heritage Foundation explained, "This is more than a policy change. It creates, for the first time, the possibility of losing one's constitutional right to possess a firearm and the potential for up to a decade in prison by a court order issued *without the individual's knowledge or the opportunity to contest it*."[9]

I could go on describing all the pork that got laid on this bill through the years and that we had to consider when it came up for reauthorization. The protections designed for women had been extended to same-sex couples in 2012. At another time the purpose of the law was even stretched to give battered, undocumented immigrants the right to claim temporary visas. And on it went. But what, I ask again, had happened to the focus on keeping women from being abused? It had been lost. The bill was weak, unclear, diluted, and misguided. For all these reasons, though I had voted for the House version of an earlier, less diluted bill, I voted against the final version of reauthorization.

I voted against it because I want a better law. I want women protected. I don't want our rights diminished and our cause to become an opportunity for every trendy social cause politicians can think of to pile on it. I want to stop violence against women. Yet along the way in DC politics, that purpose got lost.

You see that if what you really care about is protecting women and not liberal talking points, we are on the same side. It truly is possible for a congressman to vote against a bill because she wants a better one for the purpose. That's what I did.

I'm used to being attacked for my views. That comes with the job. I was surprised, though, to be attacked by someone from the music industry. I've been a strong champion of artists and the music industry in Washington. I founded the Congressional Songwriters Caucus. I worked for years helping to craft the Music Modernization Act, which improved compensation for songwriters, helped pre-1972 artists get paid by music streaming services, and recognized producers and engineers in music copyright protection. Here's what *Rolling Stone* magazine said after describing this Act: "In short, music-makers will get more money."

I coauthored the Songwriters Equity Act. I wrote, passed, and got signed into law the tax policy change that allows songwriters to pay capital gains tax instead of ordinary income tax when they sell their catalogues. I would have thought these efforts might have earned me at least a fair hearing.

I also joined Louisiana senator John Kennedy to sponsor the Support the Copyright Alternative in Small-Claims Enforcement Act. This act protects independent musicians and artists from unauthorized reproduction of their work by creating small claims copyright courts.

Then I introduced the Ask Musicians for Music Act, which modernized copyright law for radio stations and musicians. The act required radio services to pay fair market value for the music they use and put music owners and the creative community on the same level as other American workers.

And none of these efforts were something new for me. As early as 2006, *Billboard* magazine issued an election guide section that said I was a "fierce supporter of songwriters and copyright holders" and that I worked with other representatives in being "passionate activists for music creators."[10]

Yeah, I'm bragging a bit. But I'm also wondering aloud why all this service to the music industry didn't buy me a simple phone call or opportunity to explain. Still, as I say, I'm used to it. As someone once said, "If you want a friend in Washington, get a dog."

Yet the point here isn't what Marsha Blackburn had to endure. The point is that all of us conservative women will have to go through similar episodes—though hopefully not on this scale!—from time to time in our lives. Here are the keys to getting through it:

- Let conscience, truth, and the higher good always guide you in your decisions so you can answer for them confidently later.
- Have the courage of your convictions. Do the hard thing boldly without shrinking from it because it is hard.
- Take the blows of opposition graciously—even if they come from a celebrity.

- Answer your critics with your words as well as a life of integrity.
- Always be kind and hospitable to people but fierce in defense of your ideas.

That's it! Oh, and one more thing: It may not hurt to get a dog!

Chapter Nine

Public Tactics
for the Conservative
Woman

You are a conservative woman. You are beautiful. You are gifted. You are capable. You are both passionate and compassionate. I admire you. I'm glad you're in the world.

I'll tell you something else. You can't hide. You can't go about your quiet way. To be a conservative woman in this generation means you are going to stand out. People are going to notice and force you to speak up. You'll have to be ready to give a good reason for what you believe and then you'll have to give it again—on nearly every topic, answering nearly every point of view, during every kind of occasion, convenient or not. Resent it if you will, but this is what comes of being who you are.

I suggest you do what I do. Embrace it. Join me in becoming a Happy Warrior. Don't hide and demur. Give yourself to it. You'll find joy in it, and you'll find it rewarding to change minds and perhaps even change lives as you give a wise reason for what you believe and how you live.

Perhaps you'll let me help you. Allow me to suggest some broad tactics and attitudes that will help you achieve and then change your world. This is time-honored wisdom that comes out of my own experience, but that also comes down from our mothers and from the successful conservative women we all admire. Take it. Make it your own. Pass it on to others. Let's work together to build a body of wisdom that shapes the lives of conservative women as they take their stand in the world.

1. TAKE A STAND WHERE IT COUNTS

I've seen them and you've seen them, too. They are the women who are enraged about everything all at once. They are constantly taking a stand, constantly upset about one thing or another, and constantly geared up for a fight. The problem is that women like this just aren't being heard. They aren't effective because people shut them out. You don't want to be one of them. Let me quickly say that I understand their anger. I'm enraged by what women have endured through the years and much of what they are enduring now. I despise the bigotry. I despise the put-downs. I despise not just the glass ceilings but every glass floor we had to bust through to even get to those glass ceilings at the top. And the #MeToo moment? Incensed. Infuriated. Outraged. It should never have gotten to that point before we earned respect for women and girls. And, yes, I have my #MeToo stories just like most women do. I have felt that rush of adrenaline as I ran to get in my car and lock the door and as I fought to get out the door of an office. I have had to push a guy's face away from me and slap their hand when it held on to me. Yet the art of being an effective conservative woman is that you are not all angry fire all the time. You choose your battles. You vary your tone. You find the winnable wars and you fight them. You don't make yourself the kind of person whom people shut out because you are always at full volume and full threat. Take your brave stand at the right time and on the right issues and in the right manner. The cause of women needs champions in our day. I urge you to be one of them. Just be wise and tempered as you do.

2. TEAMED TOGETHER, EVERYONE ACHIEVES MORE

Think of the word *team* as an acronym. Together Everyone Achieves More. If you want to achieve and help others achieve, invite them to be a part of your team. We get further along the road to success by working together. There is an important lesson of making a difference that I saw beautifully illustrated in nature not too long ago. It seems that if a lion and a tiger fight one-on-one, the tiger will almost always win. That's just the way it usually goes. However, if five tigers fight five lions, guess who wins? The five lions. Why? It's because the lions know how to fight as a team. They work together, picking off the weak, dividing and conquering, and merging their skills. Five tigers, though, fight like five individual tigers. They don't team up or work together. So, five lions will almost always defeat five tigers, though one-on-one it is the reverse. This is an important lesson for us. Women often read about heroes like Rosa Parks or Susan B. Anthony and assume they all fought alone to achieve what they did. It usually isn't true. We are better as a group. We are more effective in teams. My "caucus of one" experience in leading the state income tax battle was backed by thousands of Tennesseans. If you get thrust into the spotlight alone, then make the most of it. Use the solitary experience to encourage others to share your goal and to be a part of your team. If you have a choice, though, work in teams. Bring together women—and sympathetic men—of diverse skills and let the synergy take you to new heights.

3. RESPECT MALE MENTORS

To hear some infuriated women speak, all men are bad. We hear this often in our society today wherever men and masculinity as a whole are being spoken of as toxic, dangerous, and damaging. Hear me. It isn't true, and saying it is true only harms the loftier purposes a conservative woman ought to be about. Let's tell the truth. Let's show some character. Whatever horrible things individual men have done, the fact is that most men are good and have only added good things to our lives. Think back on your life. What about your wonderful father or older brother? How about those male teachers or coaches, bosses or friends, who have taught us skills or helped us rise? Where would we be without them? We have to respect the men in our pasts as well as respect those men who are mentors to us today. I've already told you how much I gained from my father. He was a quiet Christian and conservative, a loving father, a courageous soldier, a tender husband, and an inspiration to me in everything I have set my hand to achieve. He was part of a battalion of men who have stood with me and taught me throughout my life. There was Mr. Farragut, who taught me science in my middle school years. He opened up universes to me. In college a professor named Dr. Roland Jones not only taught me business but told me I had sales and marketing skills I had never even recognized. Male colleagues taught me how to be a success in the Southwestern Company, and the CEO of Castner Knott, Ralph Glassford, taught me, challenged me, and allowed me to attempt great things. There are hundreds more like these men in my life, from pastors to senior politicians, from wise, older male friends to experienced statesmen. I honor them all. Yet here's the important thing: By honoring mentors past I remain open to male mentors today and in my future. It also helps me to be clear-eyed about all the marvelous men out there in the world when the deeds of toxic males fill our headlines. If you want to be effective, honor your male mentors. Honor good men. Be open to helpful male mentors in your life now so you'll be ready for the ones who come to you in the future.

4. PICK YOUR BATTLES WISELY

There is a time to fight. There is a time to insist that the right thing is done. There is a right moment for demanding a level playing field in business and society both. Don't be afraid to say you earned that raise or promotion. Don't shrink back from confidently asserting that you deserved that job and excelled in the interview. My dear conservative woman, you are neither a quota nor a talking point. You are a woman—trained, seasoned, capable, and due equality by virtue of God putting you in this world and certainly by all that you have worked hard to become ever since. When injustice happens, when you are passed over for that job that everyone knows you were perfect for, when discrimination darkens your life—that is the time for you to take a stand. Do it wisely and calmly, but do it fiercely, nonetheless. You are not just contending for yourself, though that would be reason enough. You are contending for all other women today and all of those yet to come. Be bold. Be confident. Be part of a team if you can. Be informed. Be tough. Go after what is yours. This will likely run against parts of your nature, but there are other parts you'll have to draw on to be the Battle Queen you sometimes have to be. Go for it. Millions of us are with you.

5. BE YOUR BEST (BETTER EVERY SINGLE TIME)

I want to raise your competitive spirit. I want to challenge you to fight for your best. The truth of life—and particularly the

life of a woman—is that you have to fight for mastery of yourself in order to be the BEST you can be. By this I mean Better
Every Single Time. You are going to have to prove yourself and,
yes, perhaps more so than is true of men. That's all right. Let
it drive you to be better than you would have been otherwise.
Let it drive you, whatever the sacrifice, to be the best you can
be. I'll tell you honestly that I don't resent the fact that I've had
to prove myself almost every day of my adult life. I learned
early that I always have a choice. I can let the demands society places on me push me to achieve. Or, I can shrink back in
resentment and bitterness. Thank God my whole upbringing
conspired to make me choose the first approach. The second
choice only leads to a toxic soul and a shallow life. So show 'em
what you can do! Let their expectations—even if unfair—be
the wind in your sails to move you to the greatness you are
made for. I'll end with a secret. Everyone has to prove themselves. The muscular jock has to prove he has a brain. The
beauty queen has to prove she isn't an airhead. The son and
daughter of a rich man both have to prove they are worthy
apart from the family money. There are a million examples.
You aren't alone. Dive in. Prove yourself. Be Better Every
Single Day. Use my motto: The mundane tasks can lead to a
magnificent life.

6. GIVE BACK MORE
THAN YOU TAKE

Let me pass along some wisdom from my mother that will make you more valuable in the world as well as make your life happier. Always, always, give back more than you receive. You can also say it this way: In every situation, try to leave things better than they were when you arrived. I'll tell you that it helps me to think of this in terms of service—not just because I'm in politics but because it is what my faith, my heritage, and my values teach me. I think of myself as a servant. I am ever trying to serve people and make their lives better. I'm trying to make each life I touch better. I want to serve people. I want to add value to their lives. I want anything they give me—their trust, their time, their vote, whatever—to be returned to them with greater value, just the way those pie plates my mother borrowed were always returned full of something scrumptious or beautiful. It's the key to living a life of consequence and, in my view, of fulfilling the purpose for which God put you here in the first place. Make everything better than it was before you came along. Now that is a cause worth living for! And that's the way you leave a legacy of value.

7. BE A HAPPY WARRIOR

I've already said this of myself. Now I want to commend it to you. I want you to be a Happy Warrior in your battle for noble womanhood. What will this mean? It means that you have to understand what struggle works into your life. If hardship only means loss and pain, then it is indeed something to be dreaded. But if hardship and opposition and battles of every kind make us better, give us a chance to prove ourselves, and lead to life-defining victories, then we should rush eagerly into them rather than retreat. I want to be the kind of person who has a goofy, happy, eager look on their face when hardship comes. I know it's a chance to rise. I know it's a chance to shine. Let's go! Let's do this! That's my attitude. I want you to think the same way. If you do, you'll live with greater passion, greater spirit, and greater boldness. You'll also live a life marked by victories you would never have won if you weren't a Happy Warrior. Put a smile on your face, throw back your shoulders, and let's take life on. It's what we were made for!

SUGGESTIONS FOR MAKING YOUR CASE

Now, what you've just read are some of the broad, life-defining principles that I and other conservative women have built their lives upon. They are pillars in the broader cathedral of our lives. I refer to one of these almost daily, and it inspires and emboldens me each time.

Let's go even further, though. In your life, you are going to have to defend what you believe often. People are going to call you out, challenge you, and demand you give reasons for your conservative views. Since I want you to be confident and effective at that moment, allow me to offer another list. This one is comprised of suggestions for making a case. These come from my many years of being a conservative woman under the gun. They also come from making mistakes, watching my heroes, trial and error, and having my days of victory. I trust they will help you and also help our cause as you do what you are made to do before a watching world.

1. Be Pleasant

I don't suggest you be pleasant because you don't really have a case for what you believe and so you should smile and wink as a substitute. We are trying to change minds, for heaven's sake, not flirt! Instead, I suggest you be pleasant because rage never changed anyone's mind. If you'll think about the people who have changed your thinking about anything meaningful, you'll see what I mean. It is likely you found these people pleasant, interesting, smart, and engaging, and therefore you gave their ideas a hearing. It's going to be the same with you. Be nice. Be calm. Be pleasant. This approach is disarming, and it opens people's minds to what you have to say.

2. Don't Be Angry

This is a subset of the first point but it is worth making on its own. You've watched cable news shows just like I have. You've watched the political debates we have in Washington, DC. You've seen what it looks like when angry people scream at each other. You've even seen what angry people are like when they try to be nice but really aren't. They fail. I understand that liberal policies make you want to pull your hair out. I understand that your brother may have had to shut his business down or your uncle may have been passed over for a job or your taxes are killing you and all because of liberals' harebrained schemes. I understand that it's enough to make you want to punch the first liberal you meet on the street. But calm down. Deal with your anger at home. When you step out into the world, be a Happy Warrior: Smart, fierce, but peaceful. Angry people rarely persuade the world.

3. Get the Facts

There are a lot of people in the world who think that conservatism is a mood—a greedy, grasping, resentful, angry mood perfectly modeled by Ebenezer Scrooge. It isn't. It's a philosophy of freedom. Yet since the average person today is so steeped in liberalism, you'll have to lead them to the truth—that we are all about freedom and not about control—step-by-step, fact by fact. So, you have to read. You have to memorize. You have to know some all-purpose facts. You'll have to be smart, not just in debate but genuinely smart about what you believe. I've helped you with this in these pages, but you'll need more. See the reading list I've included at the back of this book. Start there and then carry what you read into your discussions about conservatism. You'll change minds and thus lives if you do.

4. Use Three Points

When you decide to defend a position, be ready to give three key points. You are only going to have a minute or two to open a mind or get into a conversation, so have your points memorized and ready to pop off quickly. This is the kind of thing you can practice on a walk or while driving in your car. Take the top ten issues that people constantly bring up to you and master three points in defense of each of them. Memorize the details of those three points and not just the big broad statements. Then if you get a question, you'll have the facts to back it up. Doing this will make you confident, effective, and calm in the moment.

5. Ask Questions

It's called the Socratic method and it's not all you need to know about making a point, but it ought to be a tool in your toolbox. Socrates, the ancient philosopher, used to help his students arrive at conclusions by asking questions. This allowed them to discover what they believed. You can do the same. Tell Susie, for example, that the average congressional district has 650,000 people in it. Tell her that 76,000 people came across our southern border last month. Then calmly ask, "So you think we ought to absorb a whole new congressional district of immigrants every eight months in this country? Won't that over time upend our whole political system?" Since Susie is your friend and therefore not stupid, she'll realize what is going on and be open to a change of mind. Then, you are in it together! She'll join you in thinking through wise solutions for our immigration crisis. By the way, you can also use questions without providing any facts at all. I've found that liberalism is so intellectually weak that people often see this for themselves if you just graciously ask them to explain their views.

6. Use Story

Brain scientists tell us that the most efficient way for human beings to absorb facts is through story. It is easier to hear stories. It is easier to remember stories. It is easier to recall facts and details that are associated with stories. And the brain uses fewer calories in processing stories. It is also more likely that people will repeat stories than they will random facts. I can also tell you from my own experience, nonscientific though it is, that people are more likely to have their minds changed through stories. The most effective speakers I see around me every day make great use of story. They master their facts, of course, but while other speakers might just spew these facts out in a dull fashion, the speakers I admire weave facts into stories. Often I'll hear these same stories recounted afterward by other people. I sometimes have to laugh because folks who didn't even hear the original story—who heard it second- or thirdhand—will boldly retell it as though it is their own! That's how powerful stories are. It's also how you feed a movement. When you can, use stories to make your point.

7. Reach Out and Stay in Touch

You are obviously going to find yourself defending conservatism to people you will be with only once in your life. Do your best. Be kind. Leave them with thoughts that will fester after they've left you. Yet a huge portion of the folks you defend conservatism to are going to be people you have an ongoing relationship with. You want to protect this both for the value of the friendship and for the opportunity to change minds. Try not to lose the relationship over your disagreement about politics. Stay in the game. Invite them for coffee or a bite to eat. Send them a book. Develop the relational skills that go along with a philosophy of freedom and investment in people. Our best example of this is Ronald Reagan. When he was president, he fought constantly with Tip O'Neill, the then Speaker of the House. Yet when six o'clock rolled around each evening, one of them would call the other and announce that it was "after business hours." Those two old Irishmen would get together, drink whiskey, play pinochle, and keep the relationship that made the difficult business of politics a bit easier. And, yes, minds were changed and hearts were won. Good things came of this for our country. So, make your case, be determined but kind, and keep the relationship if at all possible. It will make for a richer life and a greater influence for your conservative values. And to my dear, dear friends who find their home in the Democratic Party, I am so glad you are in my life and I value your friendship.

A FRIENDLY EXCHANGE OF IDEAS

I've suggested above that you master three key points for each issue of conservatism you think you'll have to answer for. Let me help you with this. Imagine a brief conversation between

Libby, our friend who is a liberal, and Connie, a conservative. Libby issues a challenge and Connie offers three strong points in return. As you read this, you'll get a sense of how a strong, three-point response to a challenge can win the day. Hopefully you'll also be able to craft good three-point responses on other issues I haven't included here.

Health Care

Libby: I don't get your thinking about health care. In a civilized society, everyone should be able to get treatment when they are sick. Why has it become a right only for the rich in America?

Connie: Of course health care in America shouldn't be just for the rich. Nor is it today. But here is why I am not in favor of a health care system that is completely run by the government.

1. Someone always pays. There is no such thing as free government-provided health care; it is the taxpayer who is paying. Estimates from economists on providing government-run health care is in the trillions of dollars. It is just not affordable. Also, more than 160 million people would lose their employer-provided health insurance.

2. Markets serve people better. Certainly the system needs to be improved and costs need to come
   down, but the conservative position is that the best
   health care doesn't come through government control but rather through marketplace competition,
   innovation, and correction, and also through programs that work in rural areas and are run on a
   local level.

3. No one should be forced. Everyone should have
   access to affordable health care, but we should
   not force anyone to purchase a product they do
   not want at a price they can't afford. The Affordable Care Act did this and it caused a tremendous
   amount of disruption to families and to the health
   insurance marketplace. We've sure got a mess now.
   If this is what government-controlled health care
   produces, would *you* trust the government to make
   health care decisions for your family?

Immigration

Libby: Republicans are heartless and cruel. How can conservatives stand by while little kids are taken from their
parents and kept in cages at the border?

Connie: It's heartbreaking to see what's happening at our

southern border. No one could want that. But it's a crisis not of our making. Consider this.

1. We've got to stop the flow. It's a terrible situation, for sure. Did you know that hundreds of thousands of illegal immigrants were apprehended at our southwest border in 2018 alone? And many of these people were dragging children along with them. Keep in mind that these children were brought into our country illegally, and not always by their parents. The Border Patrol makes every effort to protect children and be certain they are traveling with a parent or relative, but we are in a struggle to figure out how to handle these kinds of numbers. It's not easy, but we have to plug the holes.

2. Respect the millions who are legal. We have to respect the rights of natural-born citizens and the millions of people who worked hard to get here legally, usually at great personal cost. They are proud of their position. We can't cheapen that sacrifice, and we can't put illegal entrants in front of them in the queue.

3. There are ways to get started. Conservatives believe that the answer lies in

- Securing the border
- Empowering the border patrol
- Resolving legalization for the Dreamer children
- Enforcing the laws already on the books

Medicare

Libby: Don't conservatives want to dismantle Medicare? How is that fair?

Connie: Well, that's not quite true. Here's the reality.

1. Conservatives want to stabilize both the Medicare and Social Security trust funds.

   Numbers don't lie. Medicare as it is currently funded cannot sustain itself. People are living longer and therefore staying in the system as beneficiaries much longer. For sure the idea of "Medicare for All" is not viable. The latest study by the Urban Institute, using facts from the Congressional Budget Office, shows that such a program would require $34 trillion in additional federal spending for the first ten years. That's more than the federal government's total cost for Social Security, Medicare, and

Medicaid *combined* for the same time period. Look it up. Not doable.

2. Simplify. Talk about complicated! Medicare now requires the enrollee to pay more, change providers, and then deal with both a new insurance company and a government bureaucracy all at the same time. Senior citizens want to see the system simplified and to have more choice and options. They have paid into the Medicare system all their working life.

3. We can take steps to get it in shape. Yes, it is complicated, but a conservative approach would be to stabilize the Social Security Trust Fund, and then discuss new protocols for younger workers and new incentives to reward wellness and healthy lifestyle.

Abortion

Libby: You lose me on the abortion issue. You sound absolutely old-fashioned and out-of-date when you want to refuse a woman the right to control her own body.

Connie: Well, hang on! We're not talking old-fashioned or modern here. We're talking right and wrong.

1. A "modern" society that allows the killing of an innocent life isn't modern. It's barbaric. Protecting that life isn't old-fashioned. I'm absolutely in favor of a woman controlling her own body. I also want to make certain that unborn babies have the ability to live. To say it another way, control your own body? Yes. End the life of the individual growing inside of you? No.

2. When is a life worth saving? Even aside from any belief about the value of every life, science continues to show us that babies are real human beings, able to survive outside the womb when as small as one or two pounds, or twenty-two weeks into a pregnancy. Aborting that baby is killing a human.

3. By the way, if you are a feminist, consider this: Far more girls than boys have been aborted. In fact, China is in a huge demographic crisis now because there are far fewer young women than men. Why? Their one-child policy caused families to keep boys who were thought to be able to provide for parents better in their old age and abort girls. Though that policy is ended now, China will pay for this economically for generations.

Minimum Wage

Libby: I'm concerned about the future when I think about people trying to make a living, especially those who don't have a way to further their education and are stuck at the bottom of the ladder. Do you have a problem with raising the minimum wage?

Connie: I do, and the reason is that raising the minimum wage holds out a false promise.

1. Jobs. Wage growth. Low unemployment. These are what help lift the wage rate naturally. It's important that we encourage people to get on the first step of a jobs ladder. Get a job, then get training and move up the ladder.

2. Minimum wage often works against the worker. Studies show that a mandated minimum wage limits entry-level jobs and prohibits many people from entering the workforce.[1]

3. Employers need the ability to pay a training wage. Employees need job training and skills growth. All of this, with a robust marketplace, will raise the economic level of millions. A minimum wage hike won't.

And here are a couple of extra points:

4. Dear government: Stay out of my business. Again, the federal government is not supposed to be telling every community what they can afford to pay the workers in that community. That is a state matter, in my conservative opinion.

5. Employers are people, too. What does raising the minimum wage do to small businesses? How many would have to close their doors? A flat-rate increase that more than doubles some businesses' salary outlays could hit employers in lower-pay areas in a disastrous way. In other words, a minimum wage can often have the unintended consequence of increasing poverty in some areas.

Energy

Libby: It seems to me that conservatives just want to keep us in the petroleum business in order to line the pockets of big oil. Seems like wind, solar, and electric car companies can't get a foot in the door.

Connie: I agree with you more than you know but listen to this.

1. In the future, our energy sources will be diverse. Every healthy source of energy will likely play a role. I'm all in favor of encouraging the free market to allow those advances.

2. We need to make sure petroleum companies are kept in check, but they have been and will continue to be a big part of our country's development. Where would we be right now, today, without oil? We must be fair while encouraging big oil to be principled.

3. No question big oil and big government have had too tight a relationship. I'm against out-of-control big oil *and* out-of-control big government. That's why our energy future should be created by the free market.

Environment

Libby: We have to protect the environment, but you conservatives seem to be anti-environment and anti-EPA. Is that true?

Connie: Now it's just silly to say that conservatives are against the environment. Come on! We are all for clean air and clean water.

1. We need standards, but we need to let the industries police themselves. In 2019, the United States led the world in the reduction of carbon emissions. This is because of electric energy production moving from coal to natural gas, energy efficiencies, and awareness. We need standards for automobiles (CAFE standards) that make sense. We don't want automobiles to become less safe for our families.

2. Again, it's balance. What is more important, hanging on to ineffectual laws or opening the door to development in less-advantaged parts of America? It is important that environmental agencies use common sense and clear waterways so that farms and rural areas don't flood and so that property is usable.

3. It was conservatives who started the Environmental Protection Agency and the Department of the Interior. Just an FYI, many people, like me, refer to themselves as conservationists but not environmentalists because of the differences in priorities. We need to be sure we get to the goal of clean air and water in a way that does not make energy too expensive to afford and that it does

not burden companies to the point that it drives up costs that get passed on to consumers.

Judiciary

Libby: I don't think you can anchor all of American law on the strict words of a document that is over two hundred years old. The Constitution has to be a living document. And we need judges who take society's needs into account.

Connie: Well, if we don't anchor ourselves to some solid, long-standing body of law, we'll have more of the mess we have today—law being whatever the judge says it is. Think about this:

1. We need a country based on the rule of law and judges who protect and rule by the Constitution. Interpretations of that document that are made according to the whim of the times won't protect our citizens.

2. Our Constitution is a covenant between the people and the governed. Allow the government or judges to alter the meaning of that Constitution and you allow tyranny.

3. We need to fight against activist judges who have

agendas that are undisclosed. Judges take an oath to rule by the Constitution. They should keep that oath.

Education

Libby: Our schools are underfunded and our teachers underpaid. We aren't adjusting education to meet different ethnic demographics. I think it is time we made the federal Department of Education much bigger and fund much larger schools in America.

Connie: I know what you're saying is well intentioned, but I don't think better education comes from government alone.

1. The answer for education is a free market. It should be a marketplace where innovation is encouraged and students are the first consideration. We need every kind of school in America, all competing for students by doing a better job. We want public schools, private schools, home schools, advanced academies, and every other option. This is how education can be tailored to local needs and produce a better result through competition.

2. Think about your interaction with government. Do you want education run the way other services are?

One size fits all? Take it or leave it? And all with the force of the law behind it. No! What has produced best for the U.S. from the beginning is an educational free market.

3. The United States spends just over $700 billion per year for public elementary and secondary schools, which is just about $14,000 per student.[2] That's stunning! It's even more so when you remember that we are dropping in educational achievement compared to the rest of the world, which spends far less. What we don't need is more money. We need a different system. We need innovation in the educational system. Charter schools, magnet schools. Public systems that are innovating plus parochial and private schools that are meeting the needs of students. Choice and competition will improve education.

Military

Libby: Our military is too big and too engaged around the world. We need a leaner military that we call upon less often.

Connie: No one wants to use our military one second more than we need to. However, consider this:

1. The American military needs to be the mightiest on earth. We *are* the world's policeman. We *are* the strongest nation in the world. New superpowers like China, Iran, and Russia are rising. They can only be held in check by a strong, principled U.S. military.

2. Of course military spending has to be wise and monitored, but any dollars we spend are worth it. Consider the alternative.

3. Our military expenses are growing because our military challenges are growing. We weren't doing cyber warfare twenty years ago. Times change and threats mount. We need a military to match the schemes of our enemies today.

Now, having read what Libby and Connie have to say to each other, you see how your three-part response can work. Devise responses of your own to all the issues that concern you or that you know your friends will challenge. The important thing is to be kind, informed, brief, and open to an ongoing relationship.

These are a few of the arts of being a conservative woman in this age. There are many more such arts and habits, of course, but you will craft these for yourself as you live, contend, and join the conservative women of the world in changing hearts and minds. It is a great age in which to be a woman. It is a great age in which to be a conservative. I'm excited for you. Be the Happy Warrior you long to be, and let's change our generation together.

Chapter Ten

Habits of a Lifetime

There is a television commercial I often hear playing on my TV. The jingle that accompanies it includes the words, "I want it all, I want it now." I chuckle every time I hear it. Isn't that how so many of us approach life? We want it all, all the time, at our fingertips, and always convenient.

I have learned, though, that you can't have it all and certainly not all the time. I know this is what Hollywood and Madison Avenue may want us to believe, but it simply isn't true. What you can have, though, is what you want when you need it. Now *that* is something you have control over. That's something you can figure out.

Though there are no silver bullets, no magical solutions, I

do believe that smart women can figure out how to love their families, excel at their jobs, give back to their communities, and not find themselves completely exhausted at the end of every single day. I believe there is enough time in twenty-four hours to do what we need to do in a day. The art of living is figuring out what you are meant to do and then doing it smartly.

Let's get practical. Conservative women live in the real world and want real-world tactics for achieving, making a difference, and loving well. I realize this again every time I speak to a group of young women and they ask about the disciplines and the duties—sometimes they call them "tricks"! —that allow us busy, hard-charging conservative women to create lives of impact while also crafting lives that are sane and healthy. I love teaching them what I've learned. I also love passing on what has been handed down from the generations that came before me and from the wise women around me.

Part of what allows me to be a success on the floor of the Senate, what allows me to be organized and effective when I speak or when I'm in public, is that in private—behind the scenes—is a foundation of habits that I have developed throughout my life to keep me together and keep me at peace. These habits provide what I need so I can then be focused on the job at hand.

Now let's get to it! Here is some practical wisdom and specialized advice for level-headed women who want to go after what they need in this world.

FIND MENTORS

My first recommendation to all women is to find mentors who are willing to let you learn from their experience and advice. Women who have been in the workforce for a few decades will have an amazing amount of wisdom to share with you. Don't worry. You won't become a carbon copy of them, but you will learn by watching them and listening to them as they share their hardships and victories.

Let's be honest. Conservative women face more obstacles than women on the left. Much of this is cultural. For example—and I'm being very straightforward here—I know many women who work in religious organizations and who have expressed time and again their frustration with not being able to advance in their calling because the culture of the church does not permit women to serve in senior positions. All too often, these attitudes carry over into southern community life, as well, where the leader has to be male and the secondary spots go to women. It's hard to believe this still happens in the twenty-first century, but it does. Yet this leaves a good opportunity for you. Women who have found a way to navigate this terrain, to be both successful and fulfilled in their work despite such cultural barriers, will have solid advice. Go ask for it!

STAY SAFE

I recommend that once a mentor agrees to spend time with you, don't shrink back from the tough issues. They're likely eager to help you, so go for it! One area you will want to get advice about is how they have kept themselves safe. Every woman who has been in the workforce has likely experienced a male employer or colleague who has tried to exercise either his position or his physical power over them. Words, insults, diminishment, insinuations, and even assaults have always happened and still do. Thank goodness we are in an age when you can step up, get assistance, and not fear losing your job or a contract by speaking up to protect yourself. Get good advice for this challenge from the women you seek out as mentors.

Since I've brought up this troubling subject, let me tell you some of the steps I take. At times when I have felt uneasy, I've made certain to take someone with me to a meeting, sit in the chair nearest the door, or structure the meeting with an ending time. Sometimes I even have a printed agenda to slide across the table. I've also taken a personal defense course. I don't park in a dark garage at night, and I don't walk a block or two to get to my car. When I've felt a man has said something inappropriate or acted inappropriately, I bring it up. From years of experience, I have learned that I help him if I mention that he is a better man than to have made that statement. It's like other problems: Nip them in the bud. Deal with trouble early so it doesn't have a chance to grow.

MAKE A TO-DO LIST
AND CHECK IT OFF!

We all fight the battle for personal organization and wise scheduling, so let me tell you some of the tactics I use. I start every day with a cup of coffee and a review of my digital calendar. My memory is more visual and photographic than verbal, so I like to review a graphic layout of my schedule and mentally walk through the day. Then I do about fifteen minutes of exercise. If my day is going to be without appointments, I take time to read and write. If it is a day of office work, speeches, and meetings, I am dressed and out the door well before eight a.m. Achieving women have to get an early start on their day.

I learned disciplines like this from my mother. She is still a master of time management. When I was growing up, she constantly declared her belief that if she wasted any time at all God would take that time away from her in the future. This way of thinking caused her, and certainly has caused me also, to make use of every minute.

Let me give you an example of why I am such a product of my mother's personal habits. I love keeping birthday cards and my children's drawings on the inside of my kitchen cabinet doors. Once when Mom was visiting, I opened the door to the cabinet holding my coffee cups to find a cartoon-style drawing of a prim and proper lady, hands in lap, hair in a neat bun, and sitting ramrod straight. The words in the speech bubble were, "Of course I have time. I did it right the first time." Mother had taped that there for me. How could I not be hyperorganized after having been raised by such a woman!

It also helps to be an inveterate list maker. When the kids were small, I used to say that my Day-Timer and my prayer list were my "friends" in the passenger seat of my car. Being alone while doing all the driving I had to do was a perfect time to think and pray over my day.

I also learned to redeem every spare moment. When I had little ones in school and found myself waiting in carpool lines, I wrote thank-you notes and birthday cards, hemmed school uniform pants, and repaired ripped hemlines. Your goal should be to maximize every moment available for work without being manic and without letting work time flow over into rest and personal time. In short, there is enough time in twenty-four hours to do your work and then rest, relate, and recreate. The art is to set a schedule and then not waste the time you have.

I mentioned that on days when I'm not in the office I take time to read. I fully believe in reading opinion articles and blogs, and listening to podcasts. Given my work, I also need to read bills and legislation. I make my reading work for me. Every day I try to learn something new. Every day I try to improve my writing and speaking skills by learning a new word. Every day, as I listen to hearings and news programs, I am in debate mode in my mind—crafting new arguments, turning the diamond of an issue to see a new facet.

You may have read Malcolm Gladwell's fine book *Outliers*. He describes a "10,000 hours of practice" rule that he says has led to the success of even luminaries like the Beatles. I agree with him completely. Practice does make perfect, and much practice makes history. Fill in those moments when you are tapping the steering wheel or living vicariously through someone else's social media to instead master skills that will carry you to success in your field.

COMMUNICATE CLEARLY

Some of the most famous speeches—the Gettysburg Address, the Sermon on the Mount—practiced wise word usage to make a point. People listened and they learned and those words have endured. During my time working with the Southwestern Company, I developed an appreciation of the power of skilled conversation. I had to memorize a sales talk, learn how to deliver it, and then master the art of listening to what people were actually saying. This last discipline is one of the most important I know.

You know how important it makes you feel when someone listens so intently to what you are saying that they can repeat your words back to you. You like knowing you've been heard. You like it when they engage and ask appropriate questions. Master this art.

Genuinely listen to people. Repeat back what they say. Probe a bit. Knowing you are going to repeat back what they've said causes you to open up channels in your mind that might otherwise be closed. And them hearing you say their words back to them assures them you're engaged and that you care.

The little saying my grandmother repeated a thousand times has always stuck with me. She would insist, "God gave you two ears and one mouth. That means you are supposed to listen twice as much as you talk." It is good advice. Listening well will make what you do say more meaningful, more personal, and more effective.

BE PREPARED

While my children were too young to drive and my roles were Chief Mama-in-Charge and On-Call Chauffeur, I learned to keep my car packed with water bottles and snacks, a first aid kit, a sewing kit, plastic rain ponchos from the dollar store, a couple of dry T-shirts and dry socks, and, always, jumper cables. This simple practice saved many a needless trip and proved useful a thousand times.

In fact, that box has come to be a symbol to me of those busy early days. Now I look at that plastic box that was once overflowing and notice it is only partially full. It's a sign of how time moves quickly by, a remembrance of those sweet but hectic days not too long ago. Yet it is also a symbol of the practical wisdom I inherited from my mother and grandmother that has allowed me to navigate my busy life with some degree of skill and effectiveness.

In my life today, with the kids grown and my time as challenged as ever, I don't think so much in terms of a plastic box filled with things I might need, but I do think in terms of a "virtual box." It's a box of preparation of another kind, but I keep it just as stocked as I ever did that plastic box in my car.

You see, I have the same appointments as everyone else: doctor, dentist, hair, car repair, dinner with friends, the events of my grandchildren, etc. I have to plan for these—just like everyone else. Yet today, I also have to be uniquely prepared for my work as a senator. A microphone might be stuck in my face at any moment. A staffer might call me at any time to ask me for a tweak of policy language or words to go in a speech I'm about to give. One of my colleagues might call for an immediate and detailed chat about something coming before a committee I'm on or before the Senate as a whole. I have to be mentally prepared, have to be up-to-date, have to have thoughts about every issue stirring in my mind. These days my virtual box is filled more with mental preparation than with Band-Aids, more with visualizing my schedule than with gym socks. But the principle is the same. Be prepared. Have a box. Fill it with what you need. Don't ever allow yourself to fail through lack of advance planning and preparation.

HOME SWEET HOME

There is a piece of Tennessee commonsense wisdom that says, "If Mama ain't happy, ain't nobody happy." It's true! And, yes,

I know that folks from Texas claim this saying also, but they need to get over themselves! It came from Tennessee.

Wherever it came from, the saying points to a core truth of life. If there is turmoil at home, if things are not orderly and running well, it is a basis for a huge amount of unhappiness for Mama and everyone else.

Here is the principle: Happiness springs, in part, from an organized life. In our modern world, with cell phones and iPads, this starts with your to-do list. Even if you don't keep your schedule on a digital device, do what I do. I review mine every day. I go through all the lists that I've already made for each week. I decide which items are for me to do and which are for my family, which are for home and which are for my role in Washington.

I also make a list of projects for the month and for the year. This yearly to-do list allows me to set grand goals and track my progress with a broader view that gives me perspective on how I'm doing. I find this sets me up for success and helps me keep my family on the same trajectory. It is also how I can ensure that many different projects are moving forward well and also staying in their lane so that confusion doesn't reign.

I'll tell you another virtue of this approach, but let me tell you about a friend first. She is the kind of person who takes up only one project at a time, finishes it, and then moves on to the next task. You will never find her reading two books at one time or working on multiple anything. She does one thing, she does it at her pace and to her satisfaction, and only then does she start the next task. This has always worked for her.

I'm not made that way. I feel that it is more productive to take a step forward on something when I have the opportunity, even if I have to wait months to take the next step toward achieving my goal. As we have heard all our lives, "By the inch, it is a cinch. By the yard, it is hard." My advice is to make your list, organize your work, set those goals, and get busy when the right moment comes.

Yet the important thing is to find the approach that works for you. You may be more like my friend, doing one thing at a time and then moving on. Or you may be more like me, having projects going on a lot of fronts all at once. Whatever your style, the key is to make it a success for you. Most of all, whatever your style, get busy!

Here's my most practical tactic for staying organized and living a clutter free life. And if I haven't said it already, let me say it now: Clutter drives me crazy! It absolutely pushes me to the point that I'll call a fast stop to everything going on around me. It can be clutter in the physical space, noise, or visual clutter on my computer screen. I have to clear it out in order to get things done. So, here's what I do. I bookend my day with decluttering.

I start and end my day with straightening up, throwing away, clearing things out, and giving whatever instructions I need to give in order to keep clutter from my life. I rest better knowing I can declutter first thing in the morning. I worry less about clutter during the day knowing that I'll end my working hours with a decluttering session. This frees my mind and makes me less irritated with the untidiness we all tend to create as we work. It's a tactic I've used for a long time and, believe me, it can help keep your life from driving you mad. Remember, there is a place for everything and everything should be in its place!

A final thought on this business of projects and keeping life organized. Many women, particularly high-achieving professional women, suffer from perfectionism. If they can't do something perfectly, according to the ideal in their mind, they won't do it at all. I want you to delete this kind of thinking in your mind.

The truth is that if something is worth doing, it is worth giving it the ole college try—at least initially. You can always realign a project. You can always fix it and set it on its right course. Yet waiting to start until everything is ideal and perfection is assured is a near guarantee of a messy life.

Experts say that procrastination befalls the perfectionist who can't organize their work. In other words, they have an ideal vision of what they want to have happen, but they can't get organized to reach that ideal, so they never get started. This leads to astonishing mess, ineffectiveness, and frustration.

I take confidence in the future. My attitude is "Let me get this thing started." I'll come back to it when I can. If it is off track a bit, we'll fix it. The important thing is to keep moving. Nothing gets better when it is neglected. Nothing gets better by being left alone. You start. You get interrupted. Fine. You pick up the project again. Then you adjust. You see the goal a bit differently now that time has gone by. You keep working, adjusting, and gaining new vision. That's how great things are accomplished.

So, banish perfectionism, make those to-do lists, work your plan, think in terms of both days and years (the near and the far), and trust that tomorrow will bring all the opportunity you need to get it right. This is how we get things done on a grand scale.

HAVE RITUALS

Busy people need to build into their lives the little rituals that make for productivity and order, for clarity and happiness. I'll tell it to you straight: If you don't have rituals, the winds of the outside world will turn your life into chaos. I'm certainly not saying that you have to be overscheduled and hyperdisciplined every moment. Rather, if you will build wise rituals into your life—constant, daily habits that tame your life and give you that calm sense of all being right—then you won't be as susceptible to those stormy gales that come to mess up your world.

Let me give you some examples from my own life. I'm not much for sleep. I'm basically a five-hours-a-night person, so that means I'm an early riser. First thing each morning, I have my time for coffee and my devotional reading, and then I read through my schedule. I mentally walk through my day to keep it top of mind. I scan my to-do list to see what tasks need attention that day and which tasks need a free moment of thinking time.

Exercise comes next. I fit it into that first hour. On days when I finish my work before nine or ten, I like to say that I have time to get in a bonus round. Trust me, as we age it really does get harder. We can't let working out slip from our lives. We'll pay for it if we do.

After all this at the start of the day, I'm ready to get in gear. These rituals get me in the groove to have a good day. I realize how valuable they are the few times something interrupts them. When that happens, I'm off balance and not quite at my best. My rituals are my launchpad, and a life like mine demands the right launch each day.

Rituals give me peace in the evenings, too. I get my tote bag ready to head out the door, organize my attire for the next day, and then look over the schedule and the deliverables. Finally, I quiet my soul to get a few hours' rest.

My advice? Build unshakable rituals into your life. They bring organization. They banish chaos. They set the trajectory of your life. They grant peace.

MAKE HOME A HAVEN

Chuck and I often say that our very favorite vacation is a stay-cation. The reason we can say this is that we have worked hard to make our home a refuge from the world, a protection of our love, and a place of meaningful, enjoyable work. For many years, we've shared the tasks necessary to keep our home and property up to date. While I find relief and relaxation in gardening and cooking, he enjoys woodwork and some of the heftier yard tasks that are too strenuous for me. We've discovered that this love of work at home contributes to the intimacy we enjoy with each other.

We have many happy weekends as we work on projects around our property, enjoy lunch or dinner together, and just have "us" time. Given our exceptionally busy schedules, we need this time together. Carving out these special moments has become even more important as our family has grown and we've become empty nesters. When the children were home, we often grabbed a weekend trip away just for us, or we combined a work trip with some personal time to allow for those close moments husbands and wives need. Today, dinner and conversation on the back porch is perfection.

Every couple has to find what will work for them, then make what works a priority once they find it. Your health, your relationship, your sharing in one another's lives is what makes the difference in your ability to continue to be happy together, productive in your work, and helpful to your family.

BE READY TO TRAVEL

In my work, I travel every week. I have discovered that the best way for me to cut the time needed to prepare for a trip is to keep a half-packed travel bag. Makeup, gown, slippers, and undies are always in a bag ready to go. I just add in my change of clothing and take off. No need to stress or worry that you forgot to pack your toothbrush. You know it's in there. If you are driving, be sure your car is packed the night before. Don't leave things to the last minute. That is how you end up forgetting things.

REMEMBER FAMILY GOALS

As you think about the goals you set, be sure you put your general family goals and the goals for each of your family members at the top of the list. Just as they want to be so proud of you, you want to help them take pride in themselves and achieve wonderfully in whatever arenas they have devoted themselves. I believe that every child needs one area in which they are the best at some skill. They need to hear those accolades and have that praise heaped on them by their family, friends, coaches, and teachers. Adults are no different. So, as the late (Tennessee!) writer Alex Haley would say, "Find the good and praise it." But you can do this best when you keep lists that remind you to coach, encourage, provide, and champion each family member toward the goals that are meaningful to them. Then when they reach that goal, celebrate it. Help them talk about it! If your family sets goals at the beginning of the year, then set aside time at the end of the year to discuss the goals they reached, how they attained them, what they learned, who helped them achieve them, and why they are grateful for the experience. In our family, we generally set aside time to celebrate these goals and lessons learned during the Christmas holiday season. It enables us to cheer for one another!

INVEST TIME

I fiercely believe that my husband, children, and grands don't need more things from me; they need more time from me. Living this out keeps us all grounded and connected. It also means that you have to make some unshakable commitments.

As I shared briefly earlier in these pages, I cook a good old southern Sunday lunch for our crew every week following church. Everyone shows up with a fierce appetite, ready for good food and precious time spent together. Devices are banned in the dining room. Mealtime is for eating and talking with one another, for visiting and growing in appreciation of each other. By the time the last one of us heads out the door and the dishes are cleaned, it is generally after three p.m. Still, it is all time well spent. Each of us leave with hearts full of love for those who are nearest and dearest to us.

Finding the right balance for work and family is essential. Here's a secret: I have found that the more I focus on being sure that my family is well cared for and that we are making time for one another, the better I become with time management and prioritizing. This means I have to use some of the skills I gained from my southern roots, that I create family traditions, and that I try to make every family session something memorable and sweet.

For example, given my busy work in the Senate, I long ago decided to make those family Sunday dinners exceptional. I've worked to become a pro at making that grocery list, building in time for meal prep and cooking so that Sundays are special and are a time of enjoyment, not obligation. I make certain that we allow time to set the table, bake a birthday cake, make a flower arrangement, and make sure something special happens at each meal.

Traditions are vital. Our dining room table has old bishop chairs that sit at each end of the table. If it is your birthday or if it is some other type of special occasion for you, you get to sit in the "King Chair" or the "Queen Chair." This has become a huge deal in my family and people walk in the door asking, "Who gets the King Chair this week?"

It is simple sounding, I know. Yet when we create such traditions and see them grow in importance with each generation, we build a legacy. That legacy serves to shape lives and values for generations to come in your family.

Here is one of the central truths of my life: My work, as much of an honor as it is, would be empty and pointless if I felt I prioritized it over my family. Thus, to me, our Sunday lunch ritual is literally part of the meaning of life. I urge you: Prioritize family. Value each person. Protect family time. Create traditions. Fill every gathering with a spirit of excellence and joy. Do all you can to keep your home warm, orderly, and fun. Lives really do turn on such experiences.

FIX IT

"Nip it in the bud" is a phrase I picked up from my flower-gardening mother and grandmother. They taught me that if you didn't want a plant to grow any larger than it was or to grow in the wrong direction, you would cut off the "bud," the first beginnings of new growth. It was easier to do it earlier than later. You could prevent something unwanted from getting bigger. So, "nip it in the bud," we would say.

They are brief words that carry a huge message. If something is a problem or is out of sync with what it should be, tend to the matter early. Do not let it fester or grow to be a bigger problem. In Washington, DC, some folks say this another way: "Get there firstest with the mostest." The important thing to remember is to deal with problems early and at the root.

I've seen huge disasters occur when people are cowardly in dealing with problems. Something goes wrong. The person responsible hides, wrings his hands, looks for distractions, and only takes action when forced. Usually by that time, a relatively small matter has had time to develop into something truly destructive. Be wise. Be courageous. Be early. That's the key to dealing with problems well.

I'll tell you something else important about this. Almost every employer I know is looking for people who can solve problems fearlessly and competently. They don't admire passivity. They don't want to hire excuse makers or the hesitant. They want problem solvers. They want friendly people who also know how to be aggressive in fixing problems. If you make it your habit, then, to "nip it in the bud" early and well, you will make yourself valuable and you will rise.

This is a large part of the pathway to winning what you need, and perhaps even more, all in God's time. Now, let me list here the topics and the main principles of what we've been talking about. Perhaps you'll use this as a checklist. My goal is to help you be as successful as possible, to be a together conservative woman making your unique mark in the world. Go on, girl! I'm cheering for you!

PRACTICAL WISDOM FOR LEVEL-HEADED WOMEN

FIND MENTORS
Spend a little time with someone who has walked this path already.

STAY SAFE
Don't be afraid, do think ahead.

MAKE A TO-DO LIST AND CHECK IT OFF!
Use the tools at hand and redeem the usually wasted minutes.

COMMUNICATE CLEARLY
Tune in, listen, repeat.

BE PREPARED
Take time to keep your "plastic box" ready and updated.

HOME SWEET HOME
If home isn't right, little else is. Prioritize the most important people and place in your life.

HAVE RITUALS
Build in little rituals to create productivity and order, clarity and happiness.

MAKE HOME A HAVEN
Protect your restful, restorative hours.

BE READY TO TRAVEL
Again, it's about saving time by doing it once, not a hundred times.

REMEMBER FAMILY GOALS

Remember, your family members' goals are as important as your own.

INVEST TIME

Prioritize family. Value each person. Protect family time.

FIX IT

See a problem? Nip it in the bud!

Chapter Eleven

A Hero for Us All

In 2013 I had one of the greatest experiences of my life. It was in that year that Margaret Thatcher, long a hero and inspiration to me, died. The whole world grieved the loss of the "Iron Lady." The then Speaker of the House John Boehner, who called Thatcher one of the greatest champions of freedom the world has ever known, decided to send a delegation to the great lady's funeral from the House of Representatives. He gave me the great honor of being part of that delegation, along with George Holding of North Carolina and Michele Bachmann of Minnesota.

My time in London was a sweet time of remembrance and a thrilling time of inspiration. I was struck by the great affection most of the British people held for their first female prime minister. I was also touched when during her funeral service, the crowd rose and applauded the great champion of freedom. Baroness Thatcher had passed from this life after years of retirement, but the people had not forgotten all she had done for her nation. Among those standing and applauding that day was Queen Elizabeth II. This was only the second funeral of a nonroyal nonrelative she had attended since her coronation. The first was for Winston Churchill.

One exceptionally meaningful moment for me during the funeral came when a speaker mentioned that the great woman had been guided in her conservatism by Friedrich Hayek's *The Road to Serfdom*. It had been a defining book in my life, too, and it moved me to think that Mrs. Thatcher and I had this in common. It is amazing how we feel closer to those who love the books we love, and though I had only briefly met Margaret Thatcher I felt that through the pages of Hayek's book we shared something that shaped both our lives.

She was, without question, the greatest female champion of political conservatism who has ever lived. I want to tell you a bit about her life here, because I believe in the value of heroes. They lift our vision, don't they? They remind us of what is possible, and they help us to endure what we must to go forward in our own lives as they did in theirs. As conservative women, we will come closer to being all that we are made to be if we will ponder and emulate Margaret Thatcher's example.

It is common for writers who describe Thatcher's early life to make much of the fact that she grew up living in an apartment above her father's grocery store. They speak of this as though such a thing is unthinkable, as though it is as odd as Abraham Lincoln rising from a dirt floor cabin to the presidency. I see it differently.

What builds greatness into a child is not so much where they live but what is imparted to them by those they live with. In Margaret's case, she was fortunate to have a father who both loved her and poured the highest kind of knowledge and vision into her life. His name was Alfred Roberts. He was a shopkeeper in the Northern England market town of Grantham, Lincolnshire. To some of her biographers, this sounds small and low-class. Yet Mr. Roberts was a man with an eager mind and a love for his nation. He read conservative papers and discussed the happenings of the day with his fascinated daughter. He filled his home with the words of Rudyard Kipling, whom he admired and whose poems he memorized and recited to Margaret, often for no earthly reason at all. He was a man of strong moral principles and passionate thrift who had become, though his biographers usually do not emphasize this, both an alderman and the mayor of his city. It is no wonder that Margaret said nearly all his life, "I owe almost everything to my father."[1]

She was born in 1925, which means that when World War II began for England she was fourteen. She was a young teenager during the Blitz, a girl who all her life remembered hiding under the kitchen table when the Nazi bombs were falling. She later said she defied the Nazis by finishing her homework. She also remembered taking comfort in her devotion to books and listening by the hour to the speeches of Winston Churchill on the family radio.

One of the keys to her progress in life is that she made the most of what was offered to her. She made sure she did her best in each stage of her life knowing that it would lead on to another, loftier stage. Having studied and worked hard in her early years, she then won a scholarship to Kesteven and Grantham Girls' School, where she became "head girl." She showed academic brilliance, but she also excelled in extracurricular activities. She was well-rounded, popular, and ambitious.

She won a coveted place at Somerville College, Oxford University, and eventually graduated with a degree in chemistry. During these years she had the chance to learn from future Nobel laureate Dorothy Hodgkin. When I was interviewed by the BBC just after her funeral, I mentioned that Margaret's training as a chemist meant she knew how to combine the right elements for the right solution. It was something she went on to do when she led her nation.

We should remember that she spent part of her college years enduring the devastations of World War II England and the second part in an England that was victorious but suffering horrible economic conditions. She saw that her nation was glorious and troubled, in conflict with itself and in a battle to keep anything of its historic vision. All of this had an effect on her.

After leaving Oxford, she went on to work first for a plastics company and then for another in which she tested cake fillings. For the rest of her life she had strong opinions about cakes and what went in them. She continued to work in science but also joined political clubs and societies. Public service called to her. It was the gift of her civic-minded father.

In 1949 she met and later married Denis Thatcher, a wealthy businessman, and twins were born to them in 1953. Denis encouraged her political ambitions, and his wealth gave her an advantage. She ran for Parliament in 1950 and 1951 and lost both times. She was well-spoken and energetic. She also drew media attention for being the youngest person and the only female in the campaign. It was not enough.

She did as her hero, Winston Churchill, did. She studied. She learned. She took advice. She got better. She ran for Parliament again as the representative of Finchley in 1959 and won. Speechmaking distinguished her and helped her to rise in her party. Still, she believed there were limits. She announced often and as late as 1970 that "there will not be a woman prime minister in my lifetime—the male population is too prejudiced." This says a great deal about the kind of opposition she faced and her pessimism in the face of male misogyny.

I should tell you a bit about the state of Britain at the time Mrs. Thatcher was beginning to make a name for herself. It was a mess. England was known worldwide as "the sick man of Europe." Socialism had sunk its claws into the nation and it was failing completely. For example: In 1979, the year that Margaret Thatcher became prime minister, the economy lost 29.5 million workdays to strikes. The government owned the phone monopoly. It also owned the gas monopoly, all electricity production, and most of the automobile industry along with the most important airline in Britain and most of the nation's housing. Labor unions pretty much ran Britain, and this toxic leftist brew was killing the country.

Visitors to the nation at the time found little but "paralysis and defeatism and nostalgia."[2] The country could go cold and dark during strikes. The cities were decaying, and it was not uncommon to hear stories of people who waited weeks for a simple phone line to be installed. The maximum tax rate was a whopping 83 percent. People often made purchases based on what they could deduct from this ruinous rate. American columnist David Frum recalls his father telling him of a conversation with a friend who was having a drink in the middle of the day. "You would drink wine at lunch too," the man said, "if the government were paying for it."[3]

Thatcher's political party wasn't doing a great deal to push back. It had lost much of its reason for being. She was nearly alone in her confidence that free markets and a reclaiming of British pride would remake the nation. Her politics were a combination of capitalism, patriotism, and "business-driven individualism." She was a lone voice in a country U.S. politicians jokingly called "the People's Republic of England."

She knew that while policies were important, leadership was the real crisis. Her party's leader, Edward Heath, talked about reviving England but had no idea how to pull it off. He once called a general election under the banner "Who Governs Britain?" That he made his political slogan a question rather than an assertion was typical of his hesitant, uncertain manner. This incensed Margaret, but she held her tongue and her place and kept rising through her zeal and speaking skills.

She became the secretary of state for education and science in 1970. She drew waves of opposition with her direct manner and conservative principles, but she ended up cutting costs, saving schools, while focusing on academics. People were drawn to her clear vision. Finally, she challenged Heath for party leadership and won.

It was during this time that she began a personal makeover of the kind that few politicians have the humility to undergo. She had a style of hair and dress even she called "frumpy." She got help and learned to bring out her natural beauty, to play to her strength. In later years, François Mitterrand would say that she had "the eyes of Caligula and the mouth of Marilyn Monroe." It was true but she had to learn to emphasize these and use them to her advantage.

She also had to learn to control her voice. Critic Clive James wrote in the *Observer* in 1973 that she sounded like "a cat sliding down a blackboard." The *Daily Telegraph* described her shrill tone as a "frothy contralto." Rather than shrink back in offense she took elocution lessons at a time when she was already on the national stage. When we recall her today, we remember a low, pleasant, commanding voice coming from a woman with an iconic bouffant hairstyle and dressed in tailored, feminine suits. Yet none of this came naturally. She had to face her weaknesses and overcome them, no matter how personal or embarrassing they might be. This was part of the genius—and the courage—of Margaret Thatcher.

It was as leader of the opposition that she built her indomitable reputation. During this time, the Soviets began calling her "the Iron Lady." She embraced it. In a speech to Finchley conservatives she said, "I stand before you tonight in my Red Star chiffon evening gown, my face softly made up, and my fair hair gently waved, the Iron Lady of the Western world."[4] Clearly, she knew what she was doing. Margaret Thatcher knew she would have greater heft at home the more recognized she became worldwide. She also had her eyes set on the prime minister's seat, so she began touring the United States with frequency, meeting with Gerald Ford in 1975 and then with Jimmy Carter in 1977. In 1978 she also met with Mohamad Reza Pahlavi, the shah of Iran. She did not take her foreign secretary with her. She wanted to make an impression on her own.

This was not just vanity. England was in a "winter of discontent." The economy was so weak that a member of the ruling labor party dared to proclaim, "If I were a young man, I would emigrate."[5] Many did to avoid the hardship of life in Britain at the time.

Thatcher answered these challenges in speeches with titles like "Britain Awake." She led opposition to the ruling party's failures under the banner "Labour Isn't Working." She was right, and the nation knew it. Finally, on May 4, 1979, Margaret Thatcher was elected the first female prime minister in British history. Arriving at 10 Downing Street, she cited the famous Prayer of Saint Francis of Assisi.

> *Lord, make me an instrument of your peace,*
> *Where there is hatred, let me sow love;*
> *Where there is injury, pardon;*
> *Where there is doubt, faith;*
> *Where there is despair, hope;*
> *Where there is darkness, light;*
> *Where there is sadness, joy.*

The economy was her first task and she rushed to the challenge. She cut "direct taxes"—taxes on income and wealth—and increased "indirect taxes"—taxes on goods and services. This she thought more fair, since direct taxes are unavoidable but indirect taxes aren't universal and are based on free choices taxpayers make. She also increased interest rates to slow the growth of the money supply and thus fight inflation. She cut bloated national budgets and specifically in higher education. In a pedantic and regrettable response, Oxford University made sure she was the only Oxford-educated, post–World War II incumbent to never receive an honorary doctorate from the school. Such is the payback of the political life.

The disastrous state of the economy combined with the Thatcher government's spending cuts led to riots. Members of her own party opposed her and leaked a constant stream of vitriol to the press. Calls began arising for a "U Turn." In a famous speech given in response, Thatcher said, "To those waiting with bated breath for that favorite media catchphrase, the U turn, I have only one thing to say: 'You turn if you want to. The lady's not for turning.'" It was a sly reworking of the title for the 1948 Christopher Fry play *The Lady's Not for Burning*.

Though her job approval rating—something she ignored—fell dramatically, the economy began to recover in 1982. She said she knew it would and that rolling back the "frontiers of socialism" was her goal. In her mind, this meant breaking up the control of the labor unions. She faced a massive miners' strike in 1984–1985 and knew it was a test of her resolve with unions as a whole. She held her ground. She closed mines, she used police in answer to miner violence, and still she held her ground. In time, strikes were ended, deals were made. Her tactics worked. Throughout the rest of her term in office, union membership fell by millions, and the stranglehold of unions on British life never returned to what it was when she first became prime minister.

It was the Falklands crisis that sealed her Churchillian reputation. A junta in Argentina ordered the invasion of the Falkland Islands, a British possession, in April 1982. Some at home advised her to let the little islands go. She knew that resolution would win respect worldwide. She called a war cabinet and ordered a naval task force to retake the islands. She gave orders that cost lives, and though critics screamed, England's determination ceased to be questioned. This was particularly the case when she ordered an Argentine cruiser sunk, which led to the loss of 368 sailors. Yet her conduct during the war signaled that England was back. People spoke of the "Falklands Spirit" among the British for years afterward. Thatcher became a champion to many of the working-class British people and was celebrated the world over. She won reelection in 1983 on what was commonly called the "Falklands factor."

It was during this war that the "special relationship" between the United States and Britain became tighter. Thatcher soon found herself mentioned along with Pope John Paul II and Ronald Reagan as the great champions of the free world against communism. Often, she was the spine in this relationship. This was later demonstrated when Iraq invaded Kuwait and she found it necessary to urge President George H. W. Bush to not "go wobbly." The lady was seldom for turning or retreating on any front at all.

We should remember that it was not easy being a lady in her time, not even when she was prime minster. Here's a story that confirms this. In October 1983, she was in one of the most pressing crises she would face. The United States was planning to invade Grenada, which was a part of the British Common-wealth. On the evening before this planned invasion, she was a guest at a farewell party for the outgoing U.S. ambassador. She was eager to meet with the man and discuss the matters of war and diplomacy that threatened the relationship between the two countries. She waited nearly all of the evening until dinner was done and a moment aside might present itself.

Yet when dinner ended, the women in attendance were expected to "withdraw" so that the men could enjoy port and cigars in the dining room. She never got to discuss that urgent business with the ambassador. Now, let's be clear about what happened. It was 1983, not 1783. Margaret Thatcher was the prime minister of the United Kingdom of Great Britain and Northern Ireland. And she was in the U.S. embassy at the time. Yet she, as a woman, was expected to pull away with the other wives rather than conduct urgent international busi-ness, and all so that the good old boys' club could puff their stogies alone. Such was the malignant culture she faced.[6]

Yet she endured it all with humor and grace. She never let it embitter her or turn her against men, particularly her husband,

Denis. In fact, her devotion to him seemed very out of step with the rising feminism of her day. The story was often told in London gentlemen's clubs about that evening years before when she was still a Cabinet member. Startling everyone in a meeting, she jumped up and hurried out on the streets to buy bacon for her husband's breakfast the following morning. When an associate said that there were plenty of people who would be glad to do that for her given her important work, she replied that only she knew how to do it right. She was both loving wife and feminist icon crashing through glass ceilings at will. Such was the beauty and the mystery of Margaret Thatcher.

Whatever she was at home, she was a juggernaut in her public life. William Pile, who worked with her in the 1970s, once said that "She is the only person I know who I don't think I've ever heard say, 'I wonder whether.'"[7] A biographer wrote that she was so determined that even her walk, every step of it, was decisive. She seemed to "crush and grind doubts beneath her pumps."[8]

The simple truth is that Margaret Thatcher changed the British politics of her generation and changed England for even longer. She revealed that she knew this when she was once asked what her greatest accomplishment was. She smiled and answered, "Tony Blair." Here's the joke: Blair was a Labour prime minister. He was supposed to be far left. Yet she had so moved the lines that, as one columnist has written, "Blair accepted Thatcher's changes to Britain's labor laws. He accepted the end of price controls. He accepted the privatization of industry. He accepted that government spending could not rise indefinitely. He accepted the role of the entrepreneur in the modern economy."[9]

Her service as prime minister was brought to a cruel end through party infighting in 1990. It was, she believed, a betrayal. She left 10 Downing Street in tears. She returned to Parliament as a backbencher until 1992 when she retired at the age of sixty-six.

She wrote memoirs, started foundations, made speeches the world over, and even became the honorary chancellor of the College of William and Mary in the United States. She was always a champion of her beloved conservative values. This continued when she was named a "peer of the realm" and became Lady Thatcher, a baroness and member of the House of Lords.

On the wall of an old building in Grantham, England, is a plaque bearing these words: "Birthplace of the Rt. Hon. Margaret Thatcher, M.P. First Woman Prime Minister of Great Britain and Northern Ireland." The building once contained a grocery store on one floor and a family home on the second. In that home a teenage girl read books and listened devotedly to her father recite Methodist truths, the poetry of Rudyard Kipling, and the wisdom of the conservative magazines he read daily. The girl read and practiced her piano and threw herself into her schoolwork as her father told her good British girls should do. When the Nazi bombs fell she hid under the kitchen table and finished her homework. It was her way of striking back against the fear and the evil pressing in.

―――――――――――

The life of Margaret Thatcher moves me. It inspires me. I love that as late as 1990 there were Thatcher Societies in Russia. It moves me that well-taught little girls here in the States often tell me they want to grow up to be like Margaret Thatcher. I'm delighted that the Brexit movement in England is often called the grandchild of Margaret Thatcher.

When I am being attacked, when I have my own dark nights of the soul, when I face bigotry for being a woman or take hits for being a conservative—I think of Margaret Thatcher. She is a hero to me, which means she makes me better and spurs me on. I'm grateful for her life. Later, during a visit to Cambridge for a speech, I was thrilled to visit her archives and gain even more insight into her life.

My hope is that you are grateful for her, too. My hope is that you will read further about her amazing life, absorb her deep principles, and make her leadership style part of your own. If we are still saying in a hundred years that Margaret Thatcher was the greatest female conservative leader ever, we will have missed the reason this great woman was sent to us. It was not so that we could look back and honor her. It was so that others like her might rise up. Let's do all we can to make this happen.

There is a seven-and-a-half-foot-tall statue of Thatcher in the House of Commons. It sits just opposite the statue of Winston Churchill. In 2007, when the monument was unveiled, Margaret Thatcher was there—despite her strokes and frailty and failing memory. Though friends protested, she made a speech.

"I might have preferred iron," she told the enthralled crowd, "but bronze will do."

She was ever the Iron Lady. Thank God.

Chapter Twelve

A Vision

We are living in an age of opportunity for conservative women. It is as though our times have conspired to thrust us forward. Glass ceilings are being broken worldwide. The #MeToo moment is becoming a #MeToo movement that promises to clear our path of abuse and denigration. We stand between the hard-won legacies we received from our mothers and the heights to which we can now launch our daughters.

We also live at a time when liberalism is fraying, its disproven ideas confirmed by suffering and lack around the globe. This is an opportunity for our conservative values to prove themselves once again. There are also the victories of the Trump administration. They put certainty to our ideas—the rule of law, a strong defense, low taxes, a vibrant free market, religious freedom, protection of life in the womb, a diverse educational marketplace, private health care, and pro-family policies—as valid solutions for our times.

Clearly, the day of the conservative woman has arrived. Yet we will have to be bold. We will have to be courageous. Liberalism still haunts our country and it will oppose us at every opportunity. Still, there is a world to win, and we can win it in our lifetimes if we are smart, daring, and principled.

The prize is too great, future generations too valuable, for us to hesitate. We can see our philosophy of freedom prevail, not only because it is ours but because it is true and it sets the captives free. So let us fearlessly but lovingly, intelligently but passionately, be the Happy Warriors of conservativism we are meant to be, and let us always remember the words of Margaret Thatcher: "I am in politics because of the conflict between good and evil, and I believe that in the end good will triumph."

Marsha Blackburn Reading List

1. *The Road to Serfdom: Fiftieth Anniversary Edition* by Friedrich Hayek, Introduction by Milton Friedman
2. *Atlas Shrugged* by Ayn Rand
3. *Up from Liberalism* by William F. Buckley Jr.
4. *God and Man at Yale* by William F. Buckley Jr.
5. *The Conscience of a Conservative* by Barry Goldwater
6. *Russell Kirk's Concise Guide to Conservatism* by Russell Kirk
7. *The Federalist Papers* by Alexander Hamilton, James Madison, and John Jay
8. *The Conservative Mind: From Burke to Eliot* by Russell Kirk
9. *Reflections on the Revolution in France* by Edmund Burke
10. *Margaret Thatcher: The Autobiography* by Margaret Thatcher
11. *The Conservative Heart* by Arthur C. Brooks
12. *The Road to Freedom: How to Win the Fight for Free Enterprise* by Arthur C. Brooks
13. *Capitalism and Freedom* by Milton Friedman

Acknowledgments

In the spring of 2019, Beverly Mansfield turned to me at dinner one evening and told me she felt it was time for me to write another book. We discussed this for a while and then she asked, "If you do start a book soon, what would you want it to be about and what would you title it?" That began the conversation that led to this book.

Over time, as we talked through what I would want to write, Beverly mentioned some of my ideas to her husband, Stephen, and he joined in the encouragement. Thus, this book, *The Mind of a Conservative Woman*, was born. I am incredibly grateful for their guidance and direction.

They led me to Byron Williamson and the team at Hachette Book Group, who saw the potential in the project and worked diligently, consistently, and patiently to help me move this to completion. I'm grateful beyond words.

My husband, Chuck, should be given a Ph.D. in listening to me opine on public policy. Yet he humorously tells folks that his next book is going to be titled *I Carried Her Purse*. The truth is that he graciously prefers to celebrate all the hours of toil, labor, and partnership that it took for me to pursue my dreams. Thank you!

Our children—Mary Morgan and her husband, Paul; Chad and his wife, Hillary—have both nudged me forward and pushed back when I needed correction. Often I have answered their youthful questions of "Why?" with "Because I'm the chief mama in charge and I said so!" These days, I mainly use that line on my preciously opinionated grandsons, Jack and Chase. They are completely my favorite people and I love them more than life.

I also want to thank my Senate office chief of staff, Chuck Flint, and our counsel, Jon Adame. They worked with the appropriate Senate committees and my publisher to be certain that guidelines were followed, that all *i*'s were dotted and *t*'s were crossed. I appreciate their investment in this project.

Finally, I dedicate this book to the conservative women with whom I've served at all levels of government. We have learned from one another, depended upon and propped up one another, and found a way forward that widens and opens a pathway for those who will follow us. These women have never been shown the respect they deserve for the work they selflessly do, and I am pleased to honor them here.

Notes

CHAPTER 1

1. Adam Martin, "Obama's 'Life of Julia' Was Made to Be Mocked," *Atlantic*, May 3, 2012. https://www.theatlantic.com /politics/archive/2012/05/obamas-life-julia-was-made-be -mocked/328589.

2. The survey of the slideshow "The Life of Julia" that appears in the following paragraphs is a composite drawn from these sources: Eugene Kiely, "'The Life of Julia,' Corrected," FactCheck.org, May 8, 2012; William J. Bennett, "Obama's 'Life of Julia' Is the Wrong Vision for America," CNN, May 9, 2012; Jamie Weinstein, "Top Ten #Julia Tweets," *Daily Caller*, May 3, 2012.

3. Jamie Weinstein, "Top Ten #Julia Tweets", *Daily Caller*, May 3, 2012.

CHAPTER 3

1. "Book Sellers End Sex Discrimination," *Reflector*, Mississippi State University, February 4, 1972, p. 15.

CHAPTER 5

1. Russell Kirk, *The Roots of American Order* (LaSalle, IL: Open Court, 1974), p. 672.

2. Russell Kirk, *The Politics of Prudence* (Bryn Mawr, PA: Intercollegiate Studies Institute, 1993), p. 17.

3. Kirk, *Politics of Prudence*, pp. 18–19.

4. Russell Kirk, "The Six Core Beliefs of Conservatism," *Intercollegiate Review*, July 31, 2018.

5. Russell Kirk, *The Essential Russell Kirk: Selected Essays*. Wilmington, DE: Intercollegiate Studies Institute, 2014.

6. Edmund Burke, *Thoughts on the Present Discontents*, available at https://www.gutenberg.org/files/2173/2173-h/2173-h.htm.

7. Quoted in Kirk, *Politics of Prudence*, p. 20.

8. Kirk, *Politics of Prudence*, p. 20.

9. Kirk, *Politics of Prudence*, p. 20.

10. Kirk, *Politics of Prudence*, p. 25.

11. Kirk, *Politics of Prudence*, p. 25.

CHAPTER 6

1. Edmund Burke, *Reflections on the Revolution in France*, edited by Thomas H. D. Mahoney (Indianapolis: Bobbs-Merrill, 1952), p. 102.

2. Russell Kirk, *Edmund Burke: A Genius Reconsidered* (New Rochelle, NY: Arlington House, 1967), p. 33.

3. Kirk, *Edmund Burke*, p. 131.

4. Kirk, *Edmund Burke*, p. 151.

5. Quoted in Russell Kirk, *The Conservative Mind: From Burke to Santayana* (Chicago: Henry Regnery, 1953), p. 60.

6. Quoted in Kirk, *Edmund Burke*, p. 90.

7. Quoted in Kirk, *Edmund Burke*, pp. 160–161.

8. Quoted in Kirk, *Conservative Mind*, p. 39.

9. Kirk, *Conservative Mind*, p. 61.

10. Quoted in Kirk, *Roots of American Order*, p. 448.

11. The Project Gutenberg EBook of Democracy in America, Volume 1 (of 2), by Alexis de Toqueville. Translator: Henry Reeve. Release Date: January 21, 2006 [EBook #815]. Last Updated: February 7, 2013. Chapter XVII: Principle Causes Maintaining the Democratic Republic, Part II. https://www .gutenberg.org/files/815/815-h/815-h.htm.

12. Quoted in Kirk, *Roots of American Order*, p. 447.

13. Quoted in Kirk, *Roots of American Order*, p. 30.

14. Adams Family Papers: An Electronic Archive. Massachusetts Historical Society. http://www.masshist.org/digitaladams /archive/doc?id=L17760331aa.

CHAPTER 7

1. This figure is derived from the CDCs Abortion Surveillance System FAQs, which reports 623,471 legal abortions performed in the United States in 2016. This computes to 1,708 abortions per day. https://www.cdc.gov /reproductivehealth/data_stats/abortion.htm.

2. Michael Mullen, August 27, 2010, "Mullen: Debt Is Top National Security Threat." http://www.cnn.com/2010 /US/08/27/debt.security.mullen/index.html.

CHAPTER 8

1. The original German is "Gesetze sind wie Würste, man sollte besser nicht dabei sein, wenn sie gemacht warden." It is also attributed to John Godfrey Saxe in "An Impeachment Trial," *University Chronicle* (University of Michigan), vol. 3, no. 24, March 27, 1869, https://books.google.de/books?id=cEHiAAA AMAAJ&pg=PA164.

2. Quoted in Eliza Relman, "'It Came Out of the Blue': Tennessee Democratic Senate Candidate Describes the Shock of Learning of Taylor Swift's Endorsement," *Business Insider*, October 31, 2018.

3. "Taylor Swift's Endorsement Won't Impact Race Because Her Fans Are Too Young, Huckabee Says," *Nashville Tennessean*, October 8, 2018. https://www.tennessean.com/story/news /politics/2018/10/08/taylor-swift-blackburn-bredesen-race -huckabee/1569354002.

4. *Miss Americana*, Netflix, released January 31, 2020.

5. "Blackburn Statement on Taylor Swift Documentary," https:// www.blackburn.senate.gov/blackburn-statement-taylor-swift -documentary.

6. Madeline Fry, "'Trump in a Wig': Is Taylor Swift Right about Marsha Blackburn?" *Washington Examiner*, February 3, 2020.

7. https://www.govinfo.gov/content/pkg/USCODE-2011-title42 /html/USCODE-2011-title42-chap136-subchapIII.htm.

8. https://www.congress.gov/bill/115th-congress/house-bill/6545 /text#toc-H1F75893350EB4AE58652E817E7A502F7.

9. Thomas Jipping, "Serious Flaws in the Violence Against Women Act Reauthorization Bill," *Report: Crime and Justice*,

Heritage Foundation, July 22, 2019. Italics are in the original.

10. Election Guide, *Billboard*, November 2006. https://books
.google.com/books?id=Pg8EAAAAMBAJ.

CHAPTER 9

1. Congressional Budget Office, https://www.cbo.gov/publication
/55681.

2. National Center for Education Statistics, https://nces.ed.gov
/fastfacts/display.asp?id=66.

CHAPTER 11

1. Henry Chu and Patt Morrison, "Margaret Thatcher Dies at 87;
Britain's First Female Prime Minister," *Los Angeles Times*, April
8, 2013.

2. David Frum, "Why Thatcher Matters—More than Ever,"
Atlantic, February 18, 2016.

3. David Frum, "How Margaret Thatcher Saved Britain and
Changed the World," *Daily Beast*, April 8, 2013.

4. "Speech to Finchley Conservatives," January 31, 1976,
Margaret Thatcher Foundation.

5. Andy Beckett, *When the Lights Went Out: Britain in the
Seventies* (London: Faber and Faber, 2009), p. 172.

6. Frum, "Why Thatcher Matters."

7. Chu and Morrison, "Margaret Thatcher Dies at 87."

8. Frum, "Why Thatcher Matters."

9. Frum, "How Margaret Thatcher Saved Britain."

About the Author

MARSHA BLACKBURN is the first woman ever elected to the United States Senate from Tennessee. Before ascending to that role, she represented Tennessee's Seventh District in the United States Congress for sixteen years and served as a state senator for four years. She is known for her mastery of the political process, her fiery defense of her principles, and her wit. Senator Blackburn is a mother to two, a grandmother to two, and wife to her husband, Chuck, to whom she has been married for more than forty years.